D1624669

PUTTING A FACE ON GRACE

PUTTING A
FACE ON
GRACE

RICHARD
BLACKABY

Multnomah® Publishers *Sisters, Oregon*

PUTTING A FACE ON GRACE
published by Multnomah Publishers, Inc.

Published in association with the literary agency Wolgemuth & Associates, Inc,
8600 Crestgate Circle, Orlando, FL 32819

© 2006 by Richard Blackaby
International Standard Book Number: 1-59052-481-0

Image by Jo McRyan/Getty Images

Scripture quotations are from:
The Holy Bible, New King James Version, © 1984 by Thomas Nelson, Inc.

Multnomah is a trademark of Multnomah Publishers, Inc.,
and is registered in the U.S. Patent and Trademark Office.
The colophon is a trademark of Multnomah Publishers, Inc.

Printed in the United States of America

ALL RIGHTS RESERVED
No part of this publication may be reproduced, stored in a retrieval system,
or transmitted, in any form or by any means—electronic, mechanical,
photocopying, recording, or otherwise—without prior written permission.

For information:
MULTNOMAH PUBLISHERS, INC.
601 N. LARCH ST.
SISTERS, OREGON 97759

Library of Congress Cataloging-in-Publication Data
Blackaby, Richard, 1961-
    Putting a face on grace : living a life worth passing on / Richard
Blackaby.
        p. cm.
    ISBN 1-59052-481-0
    Includes bibliographical references and index.
    1. Christian life. 2. Grace (Theology) I. Title.

BV4501.3.B532 2006
248.4—dc22

                                                                2005026833

06 07 08 09 10 11 12—10 9 8 7 6 5 4 3 2 1 0

To my parents
who not only taught me about grace
but continue to model it before me daily.

CONTENTS

FOREWORD

by Henry Blackaby

REVIVAL TARRIES for the lack of people experiencing and expressing God's grace. God intended that His grace would be life transforming. To truly know God's grace is to pass it on to others. Withholding grace from others begs the question whether one has any idea of the magnitude of God's merciful love.

This book is both exquisitely practical and intensely convicting. It blends the "knowing" and the "doing" into a vital message that must be taken seriously by both Christians and non-Christians.

It is not too late for revival if God's people will fully receive and dispense God's grace. The wisdom found on these pages is a timely step in the right direction.

ACKNOWLEDGMENTS

SPECIAL THANKS to my wife and soul mate, Lisa, who has faithfully edited everything I have ever written since our marriage. Thanks, Leese, for being thorough and honest and for all the fun little notes you wrote in the margin that no one but me will ever see. I love you!

God blessed me with a team of special friends (Ross and Phyllis Lincer, Lou Leventhal, Hermann Brandt, and Barry Nelson) who squeezed time into their full schedules to read through the manuscript and offer wise and insightful suggestions. You all know me well and were able to help me express the things God laid on my heart. Your friendship and encouragement is one of God's many grace gifts to me.

INTRODUCTION

I ONCE HAD A UNIVERSITY professor who performed a mischievous experiment on his class. He gave a midterm exam, marked the tests, and recorded the grades. Then he randomly chose eight exams and on the front page of each one he wrote a number 10 percent *lower* than the actual grade he had already recorded. On another eight tests, he put a grade 10 percent *higher* than the students' actual scores. He returned the exams at the close of the next class. The following week, he confessed his scheme and reported that eight of the sixteen students had contacted him to point out his "mistake." You can guess which eight they were. Those who received more than they deserved were conspicuously silent. Not one recipient of the bonus 10 percent had spoken up, but all eight shortchanged students were prompt to lodge a grievance. That's human nature.

We gladly accept what is freely given, but we are wary of those who would take advantage of us.

There is a story told about William Fleming, a successful Texas businessman. He explained to his pastor that since he was now earning millions of dollars in oil revenue, he could no longer afford to give a tithe (10 percent of his gross income) to God through his local church. He explained that his assets were not liquid and then delved into tax implications. His pastor sympathized and told Fleming he could see the dilemma. The pastor then promised to earnestly beseech God to reduce Fleming's income to a level from which he could once again afford to tithe. Fleming got the point. He eventually became a generous philanthropist who enjoyed giving millions of dollars to numerous Christian causes.

Many of us can relate to Fleming's conundrum: the more we have, the harder it becomes for us to give. And money isn't the only area we struggle in. I have the privilege of traveling to scores of cities and numerous countries. I meet hundreds of wonderful Christians who have been marvelously saved by God's grace. They testify to God's patience in pursuing them as they pursued sin. They tell of God's loving persistence though they continually rejected Him. Yet, without realizing it, many of these grateful believers withhold from others the very gift they so readily continue to receive—the gift of grace.

Many believers withhold from others the very gift they so readily continue to receive— the gift of grace.

No windfall or inheritance comes close to the blessing we receive when we accept God's free gift of eternal life. You would think after receiving such undeserved grace, we would be generous toward others. Yet the opposite is often true. Christians can be the most graceless, judgmental people on earth. This is the paradox of graceless Christians.

Recently I visited with a fine couple after a service where I was the guest speaker. I had preached several times at their church and we had struck up a friendly relationship. They are dear people, with a glorious testimony of God's faithfulness to them. That Sunday, my sermon was about God's grace. I shared how God doesn't focus on unimportant things, but rather He lovingly helps us become more like Christ.

After the service, this couple immediately approached me. They were both visibly shaken. "You were God's messenger to us today," they said, and they told me their story. Their teenage daughter was causing them great frustration, and the situation had reached a boiling point. They had determined to confront her that very day to insist she move out until she "got her act together." They were preparing for a showdown as soon as they got home.

One could just picture the scene: this dear man and woman up against a petulant, defiant, multipierced, tattooed girl in a black tee shirt peppered with skulls and crossbones. But I had met their daughter. She was nothing like that. She had graduated from high school that spring. With half the summer gone, she still did not know which college to attend nor did she have a clear direction for her life.

The reason they had not confronted her sooner was that she had been on a mission trip to Central America with her church youth group. Their daughter was a vivacious extrovert. She loved her church and she enjoyed doing mission work. She was somewhat disorganized and allegedly not a neat freak, but she was a great kid. She didn't use drugs. She wasn't hanging out with the wrong crowd. She loved Jesus and wanted to serve Him. She just didn't know how or where yet.

That morning God gently lifted the veil from her parents' eyes. They realized they had become so absorbed in their daughter's shortcomings they were oblivious to the truth that in all of the important categories, she had made them very proud. The mother emotionally admitted, "If you had not preached on what you did today, we would have gone home and thrown our daughter out of our house." That fall their daughter enrolled in a Christian university and continues to faithfully serve the Lord.

These were not bad parents. They were wonderful Christians and solid church members. They had simply lost sight of grace. While they eagerly accepted all the grace God was showering on them, they had denied grace to their own precious daughter. They were stunned by what they had almost done. But they shouldn't have been. It happens all the time. I could tell story after story about good people who somewhere along their spiritual journey lost the wonder of God's grace.

I could tell story after story about good people who somewhere along their spiritual journey lost the wonder of God's grace.

To be honest, I could recount many stories about how *I* have been stingy with God's limitless grace. At times, I, too, have been a graceless Christian. I have received so much, and yet it pained me to give even a little. I have relied daily on God's forgiveness and mercy, yet I blithely looked the other way when people needed grace from me. I am writing this book not because I am an expert on grace, but because I have been a major recipient of God's forgiveness and favor. Over the years God, in His grace, has redeemed my failures and taught me about His love and grace. These are the lessons I want to pass on to you.

I want to share the phenomenal way God can renew your heart and mind to make you a conduit of grace. You can become a generous grace-giver in ways you never imagined. And you will find yourself sharing Christ's love with people who have never been on your radar screen. That's what being Christlike is about. As you read this book, open your heart to the metamorphosis God wants to perform in your life.

Note: At times throughout this book, people's names have been changed to protect their privacy.

1

THE PARADOX OF GRACELESS CHRISTIANS

OMETIMES MY TRAVEL schedule can get pretty stressful. Last year I was flying to Jackson, Mississippi, to preach at a church, passing through Denver on my way. When I arrived in Denver, everyone in the airport seemed to be in a bad mood. There were frowns on most faces. As I approached the gate to board the plane, I heard an announcement that the gate had been changed to one at the opposite end of the terminal. A small herd of disgruntled passengers wearily arose and trudged to the new gate. They were not happy travelers! One couple was having a heated argument. Two sets of parents were snapping at their children. One elderly man was muttering to anyone who would listen (no one was).

Then the agent announced that the gate had been changed once again. Now the crowd was in danger of degenerating into a lynch mob. By the time I arrived at the third gate, no seats were available in the waiting area. I stood leaning against a wall. Suddenly there was another announcement, but this one was for *me*. "May I please have your attention? Would a Richard Black-Baby please see the ticket agent?"

Now *I* was annoyed. These airline employees truly were incompetent. They couldn't even pronounce a simple English name like *Blackaby*. I marched up to the desk. "I'm Richard BLACKABY," I said. "That's 'Bee' as in bumble." The agent asked for my ticket so I handed it to him. Without batting an eye, he ripped it in two. "We need your seat," he explained matter-of-factly. Then he handed me a business-class ticket. "I hope you don't mind if we upgrade you to business class," he said with a smile. Suddenly the sun came out and I could hear birds singing. Everything was going to be okay. "Richard Black-Baby at your service," I said. "And God bless us, every one!"

"I hope you don't mind if we upgrade you to business class," he said with a smile.

The moment they announced that business class could board, I scurried to find my place. It was a large, comfortable seat, and I quickly settled in. I watched exhausted travelers and bedraggled parents muttering instructions to their kids as they made their way to the cramped recesses at the rear of the plane, and I lifted a prayer of thanks to God that I did not have to pass "behind the veil" with them. We had a cheerful flight attendant who continually asked, "What else can I bring you?" I had already gulped down a soft drink, a bottle of water, and a cup of coffee before we even taxied to the runway.

As soon as we were airborne, our Johnny-on-the-spot flight attendant was asking me whether I would prefer sirloin tips or salmon. Both were a far cry from the offerings a few rows behind me: stale pretzels or no stale pretzels.

As time passed I overheard a disturbing conversation between a woman across the aisle and our flight attendant. This passenger had been called to the podium shortly after I was and she, too, had been upgraded. It seemed she was not as enamored with her good fortune as I was. When told what brand of coffee they served on the plane, she said, "Oh, I can't stand that stuff!" When the flight attendant told her he did not have the necessary ingredients to mix the drink she requested, she snapped, "Well, what *do* you have then?" When she took her first bite of salmon, she spit it out, complaining it wasn't fresh.

I couldn't believe my ears. I wanted to stand up and say something to her. I knew she should be choking down twisted little pieces of salted, baked dough, not eating salmon. I knew the overworked flight attendants in the economy coach were far too busy to give her the polite attention our smiling steward was giving us. I wanted to ask this woman, after all that had been done for her, how she could possibly complain. How could she be demanding and impatient with someone who was trying so hard to help her? Of course I didn't say a word. I had already watched her make mincemeat out of our courteous flight attendant.

Upgraded Christians

Christians are people who have been more than upgraded. We were headed to one destination and God rerouted us to a vastly better place (Ephesians 2:3–10). We were traveling with limited, perishable resources. Now we have the Holy Spirit guiding us to receive everything God has prepared for us (1 Corinthians 2:9–16).

We were alienated from God; now we are children of the King, with access to all the treasures of God's kingdom (Ephesians 2:7, 13). We were living in defeat; now we are assured of victory. We used to rely on our own strength and wisdom. Now almighty God walks with us day by day. We used to stumble in darkness; now we walk in the light. We were spiritually dead and now we are alive. Christianity is truly a miracle of enormous magnitude.

GRACELESS CHRISTIANS

Yet, like my malcontented fellow traveler, many Christians have lost the wonder of what God's grace has done for them. Tragically, they have fallen into a debilitating sense of self-centered entitlement, behaving as if God exists solely to serve them and to make them happy. These people forget how hopeless their situation was before God rescued them by His grace. They overlook the fact God is not obligated to redeem them or to walk with them daily or to answer their prayers or even to continue loving them when they act intolerably.

While "Amazing Grace" may be a popular hymn among millions of believers, it is not the lifestyle of choice for many.

Our generation may be one of the most self-centered in history. There is a chronic condition in our society that is far more widespread than is generally acknowledged. It affects most Christians. Its causes are difficult to understand but its symptoms are obvious. And it seems to be contagious. It is perplexing to witness. It is as inexcusable as it is pervasive. It contradicts the very purpose of Christ's death on the cross. It is the paradoxical epidemic of graceless Christianity.

A baffling reality is that the richest people in the world can be some of the stingiest tightwads. Those who have the most can be the least willing to show generosity to others. While "Amazing Grace" may be a popular hymn among millions of believers, it is not the lifestyle of choice for many. Consider just a few examples of graceless Christians:

- People complain they "got nothing out of the service" because the worship leader did not schedule any of their favorite hymns.
- Members angrily leave the church because the pastor changed the format of the service.
- Believers become resentful toward God because He did not answer their prayers the way they wanted Him to.
- People leave the church auditorium promptly at the twelve o'clock hour whether the pastor is finished speaking or not.
- Church leaders are slandered by people who have been "overlooked" for prominent positions.
- Two Christians refuse to forgive one another.
- Members leave the church because the pastor talks too much about giving.
- Christian parents refuse to speak to their adult son or daughter because he or she did not heed their advice.

A Graceless Prodigal

Do you know people who have forgotten how much they depend on God's grace? They are all around you. John grew up in a Christian home. He professed faith in Christ as a child and regularly attended church with his family. But during his teenage years, he became a full-fledged rebel. He pursued whatever pleasures the world offered. He indulged in drugs and drinking and he ran around with the "bad" crowd. He broke his parents' hearts. They reasoned with him and argued with him. They pled with him and prayed for him. Yet it seemed he would never abandon his destructive ways. After several years of hard, wild living, he finally hit rock bottom and came to his senses, turned to God, and returned to church. John was back, with a vengeance.

This former prodigal became the most faithful church member. He had his family in church at every opportunity. But a strange thing happened to John in his return to God—he forgot about grace. He became a legalist. He was judgmental toward those who did not measure up to his standards of righteousness. He would frequently chastise his pastor for not using more scripture in his sermons or for not preaching vehemently enough against sin. He was vocal in church business meetings, freely pointing out where he felt the church and its members were in error. Some people refused to serve on church committees because they feared John's interrogations during congregational business sessions. John spent Sunday afternoons dissecting the church and its members, exposing their shortcomings to his family.

There was trouble at home, too. John ran his household with an iron fist. He had seen firsthand the pain caused by teenage rebellion, so he aggressively prepared for that eventuality with his own kids. He established a formidable set of rules and curfews along with strict punishments for infractions. His children discovered they could never fully please their father. Always afraid of letting down his guard, John was vigilant to be firm and authoritative with his kids. As John's children became teenagers, they responded to his domineering parenting style by concealing their struggles and failures from him. Even when John's daughter was flunking out of university, she pretended all was well to avoid her father's wrath. John's children knew better than to expect grace from him.

In his youth John had been a party animal; now he was all business. His wife dutifully agreed with him, but his marriage was joyless and sterile. Their home was filled with anger and disappointment. Even John's relationship with his parents altered. They used to plead with him to return to the Lord; now their son condemned their lackadaisical religious practices and criticized their "weak" theology.

John had experienced a 180-degree transformation. But he had turned from his stubborn, carnal, bull-headed ways into a stubborn, bull-headed Christian. He once rejected his parent's faith; now he piously discounted everyone's opinion but his own. This once intractable prodigal now believed he might be the only truly righteous member in his church. He once cared nothing about theology; now he was the self-appointed chief of the orthodoxy police. John had changed alright, but not as much as he thought.

This once intractable prodigal now believed he might be the only truly righteous member in his church.

What happened? John lost sight of grace. To be more specific, he lost sight of the grace *he* had received over the years. He overlooked the copious tears his parents had wept as they prayed for him night after night. He forgot about his blasphemous comments and his cavalier rejection of God even as the Lord lovingly pursued him. He minimized the numerous occasions where people forgave him. He felt uncomfortable, even embarrassed, when reminded of his rebellious past. After all, that was then, and now he was a devout Christian. God had forgiven him, so why belabor the point?

Un-Christlike Christians

John's story exemplifies the malady of countless believers. We have enjoyed a generous outpouring of God's grace, yet we are stingy about sharing grace with others. You would think someone who freely receives forgiveness from Holy God would be eager to forgive others. Surely one who has experienced God's longsuffering will readily show patience to others. But why don't we? Christ's followers, of all people, have known mercy and grace firsthand. Yet Christians are often characterized by judgmentalism and intolerance rather than mercy and compassion.

The Grateful Sinner (Luke 7:36–50)

Jesus witnessed this enigma firsthand: Simon, a Pharisee, invited Jesus to his home for a meal. Simon was an influential leader in the community, one of the religious elite. This was a notable occasion—Simon was inviting Jesus to mix with the "Who's Who" of local society. Or rather, he was offering his colleagues access to the current religious celebrity. Perhaps they all watched eagerly to see if Jesus would perform one of His famous miracles. Some were probably pondering difficult questions they might pose to their guest, matching their theological expertise against this relative upstart.

Almost unnoticed, a woman slipped into the house. Those present would immediately recognize her as a notorious sinner. She found Jesus reclined at the low Middle Eastern table and stood sobbing behind him. Her tears splattered onto His feet making water marks in the dust that had collected. Then she unfastened her long hair, a disgraceful act in that society, and humbly wiped Jesus' feet with it. She took an alabaster flask of expensive perfume and poured the fragrant oil over Jesus' feet, filling the room with the sweet aroma. The woman continued to weep as she bent to kiss the feet of Jesus.

Simon did not comment aloud about what was happening, but his mortified expression communicated his displeasure. Jesus broke the uncomfortable silence and addressed Simon's unspoken question with a story.

He told of two men who fell into debt. One owed fifty denarii, the other five hundred. A denarius was roughly a day's wages for a common laborer, so the one man owed his earnings for a month and a half of work. The other was indebted for a year and a half's pay. When neither was able to cover his debt, their creditor forgave them both. Then Jesus asked: "Tell me, therefore, which of them will love him more?" The answer was obvious. "I suppose the one whom he forgave more," answered Simon.

Then Jesus pointed out that since His arrival at Simon's home, no one had cared for His needs. Simon had not provided for Jesus' feet to be cleaned, as a conscientious host usually did. Yet the outcast woman had cleansed Jesus' feet with her own hair. Simon had not greeted Jesus with a customary kiss on the cheek, yet the woman had continually kissed His feet. Jesus made His point: "To whom little is forgiven, the same loves little" (v. 47).

When you fail to recognize how much God has given you, you will not live a life of gratitude.

What was Simon's problem? Unlike the fallen woman, he had not committed heinous, public transgressions. Since he did not see himself as "one of them," Simon felt little compassion for those who were so obviously sinners. Simon's myopia to his own sin made him oblivious to how much he needed God's grace. He did not comprehend his many reasons to be grateful, so he did not live a thankful life.

Simon's problem was a lack of awareness. He was truly ignorant of his own needy condition. Scripture says such a lack of awareness may be the result of a hardened heart (Mark 6:52). When you fail to recognize how much God has given you, you will not live a life of gratitude.

PRINCIPLE 1: The more aware you are of your need for God's grace, the more generous you will be toward others.

Arrogance in the Temple (Luke 18:9–14)

Two men entered the temple. They represented the social extremes of their community. One was a Pharisee, known for his religious practices and scripture knowledge. Pharisees were usually treated with deference as they were considered religious experts of their day. The other man was a tax collector, making his living by perhaps the most despised profession in society. This man would be considered a traitor, a thief, and a liar. Fellow citizens would have detested him, refusing to socialize with him or to show him the most basic courtesy.

The conduct of the two was a study in contrasts. The Pharisee stood tall in a prominent spot and began to thank God for making him such an outstanding man of piety. With disdain he noticed the tax collector and expressed his thanks to God that he wasn't like *that* sinner. Then he listed all the righteous deeds he routinely performed in God's name, including tithing and fasting (two practices particularly indicative of religious fervor).

Meanwhile the tax collector was also praying, alone in an inconspicuous place. He was too ashamed of his sinful life to look heavenward. As he beat his breast in sorrow and repentance, he cried out from the depths of his heart, "God, be merciful to me a sinner!" This man knew he deserved only one thing from God—condemnation. In humility and brokenness, the tax collector could say nothing more to God than "Have mercy!"

Jesus said the one who truly sees himself as a sinner before God and seeks His mercy is the one who finds forgiveness. The one who thinks of himself in no need of grace goes away unforgiven.

PRINCIPLE 2: A true understanding of your daily dependence on God's mercy causes you to be humble toward God and others.

Frugal Forgiveness (Matthew 18:21–35)

The disciple Peter was never shy about voicing his opinions or concerns. Apparently he had some questions about forgiveness. Maybe there was someone he was struggling to forgive. Middle Eastern codes of honor demanded just recompense for every offense committed. The Jewish religion specified a traditional number of times a person was to forgive another—three times. However, Peter, perhaps wanting to be generous and impress Jesus, proposed seven as a possible number of times people should extend forgiveness. The number seven implied completeness in Peter's culture. Peter was likely taken aback by Jesus' response: not three times, not seven times, not even seventy times, but an unlimited number of times (seventy times seven).

To help Peter grasp the point, Jesus told this story. A king had many servants. One of them grew indebted to him for ten thousand talents. A common laborer earned one denarius per day, and a talent was worth roughly six thousand denarii. Doing the math, this man owed ten thousand talents, which equaled sixty million days' wages. One didn't get into such arrears by simply asking for an occasional advance on his paycheck. A person became this indebted through irresponsible or dishonest behavior. Obviously the impoverished servant didn't have sixty million working days left in his life to repay his debt. His situation was hopeless. So he threw himself at the king's feet and begged for mercy. He promised to somehow pay back his debt even though it was clearly impossible. The man and his family deserved to spend the remainder of their days laboring in bondage as lowly slaves. He and the king both knew it.

The king responded with the sweetest words imaginable. "Your debts are forgiven." The servant must have been dumfounded. No statement could be more exhilarating or welcome than this. He left the king's presence a free man, the burden of crippling, insurmountable debt gone instantaneously. His past failures were behind him. He had a fresh beginning. How would he live the new life he had received?

He immediately sought out someone who owed him one hundred denarii and demanded prompt payment. His fellow servant begged for time to repay, using the same plea he had used. But this time mercy was not forthcoming. The unforgiving tyrant threw his fellow servant in prison until he repaid every last cent he owed. While the man languished in prison, his family would suffer as they struggled to survive while slowly repaying this small debt.

Word reached the king of this cruel deed. He summoned his hard-hearted servant to reappear before him, only this time he condemned the man, consigning him to a dismal prison where torturers would torment him until he paid his debt in full. Unwillingness to forgive led this man into bondage.

PRINCIPLE 3: If you are truly grateful for God's forgiveness you will be quick to forgive others.

The truth is that our behavior clearly communicates our understanding of God's grace in our lives.

- If we grasp the enormity of God's extravagant grace toward us, we will gladly give generously to others.
- If we are truly broken and humbled by our own sinfulness, we will not focus on the sins of others. Rather, we will be motivated to humbly serve them.
- We will forgive others—whether they deserve it or not—to show our gratitude to God. After all, that's what He did for us.

SPIRITUAL SPONGES

Most of us fail to see the disparity between what we have and what we give. Why do so many Christians glory in God's amazing love toward them and yet refuse to extend grace and forgiveness toward others? They do not understand the extent of God's grace and the magnitude of their need for it. They are like spiritual sponges soaking up grace to the saturation point. Yet you have to put the squeeze on them to get any back out.

STINGY RICH PEOPLE

Richard Phillips earned a large income as a senior associate for the British law firm, Baker and McKenzie, the world's fifth largest legal firm. On May 24, 2005, he had lunch with one of the company's secretaries, Jenny Amner. During the meal, Ms. Amner accidentally spilled ketchup on Phillips's trousers. The next day Phillips sent her this e-mail: "Hi Jenny, I went to a dry cleaners at lunch and they said it would cost four pounds to remove the ketchup stains. If you could let me have the cash today, that would be much appreciated."

Ms. Amner did not respond immediately because she had to take a sudden leave of absence due to her mother's critical illness, death, and funeral. So Phillips left a note on her desk emphasizing his need for immediate reimbursement of his expense. Nine days later, she returned to work and responded with her own e-mail: "With reference to the e-mail, I must apologise for not getting back to you straight away but due to my mother's sudden illness, death and funeral I have had more pressing issues than your four pounds.... Obviously your financial need as a senior associate is greater than mine as a mere secretary."

The e-mail spread throughout the law firm and ultimately found its way onto the Internet. People were incredulous that anyone with such enormous financial resources could be so stingy toward others. Some offered to take a collection to help cover the four-pound expense. But Ms. Amner offered to pay the debt herself. Reading about this incident begs the question, how could a person with so much be so miserly? Sadly, while the story may seem extreme, the mindset is prevalent even among Christians.

No, Not One

The Bible doesn't paint a very attractive picture of human nature:

> "There is none righteous, no, not one.... There is none who does good, no, not one. Their throat is an open tomb; with their tongues they have practiced deceit; the poison of asps is under their lips; whose mouth is full of cursing and bitterness.... Destruction and misery are in their ways; and the way of peace they have not known. There is no fear of God before their eyes." (Romans 3:10–18)

Most people think they are basically good, and they assume God agrees. But Scripture is clear about what God sees. There is *no one* who naturally does good. *No one* is inherently kind and unselfish toward others. We all inherit a self-centered view of life. For Christians, this should not be big news. We know that to be born again we must first acknowledge our sinful nature. However, what many Christians fail to recognize is that being forgiven does not automatically free us from being self-centered. That's why Jesus insisted that anyone who wants to be His disciple must deny himself (daily), pick up his cross, and then follow Him (Luke 9:23).

Many Christians fail to recognize that being forgiven does not automatically free us from being self-centered.

This is where the Christian church has been vulnerable for centuries. Christians erroneously assumed that once they were believers, their thoughts and words were acceptable to God. Those outside the Christian faith can see the flaw in this thinking. What is traditionally the greatest complaint by unbelievers about the church? "It is full of *hypocrites*." The church is filled with people who claim to be children of God but sometimes they live like children of the devil. This fact prompted the apostle Paul's exhortation to "work out your own salvation with fear and trembling" (Philippians 2:12). Paul knew a godly character does not happen instantaneously. Salvation is instant but becoming like Jesus is a process. It is something a person intentionally embraces and pursues.

Conclusion

I like to be a positive person. I try not to dwell on the negative. So far, this book has presented a pretty dismal assessment of people in general and Christians in particular. But now comes the best part. I hope to help you identify areas in your life that have not yet been thoroughly sanctified by Christ. I hope to share truths that will encourage you to grow as a person of grace. I pray this book will motivate you and help you learn to talk and act more like Jesus. God can transform your life so you give hope and blessing to others. This is not only possible, it is God's desire for you and for me.

Now that we've examined the problem, let's go on to the solution. Let's discover how God intends to transform us and to make us His conduits of grace to others.

2

GRACE: EXPRESSING
GOD'S HEART

WHEN I WAS A PASTOR, I used to take Thursdays off to spend time with my wife, Lisa. We would usually go for coffee and a muffin and get caught up on the week's events while our kids were in school. I thoroughly enjoyed those getaways. Our time was always limited, though, because our kids came home for lunch. So, as soon as they went off to school in the morning, we raced off on our date.

One Thursday Lisa asked if we could make a quick stop before going to our favorite coffee place. She had a 50–percent–off coupon for a frame store and she had a picture to be framed. I was unenthusiastic. With only a brief time to spend together, I was not excited about squandering it in a shop with my wife debating over which mat matched best with which frame. However, Lisa was eager to get this job finished and she promised it would not take long.

Looking at the coupon we saw the store did not open until 10:00 a.m. I knew that by the time we were finished, we would have little time left before the kids got out of school at noon. Trying to be agreeable, I said, "Well, let's get there a little early so we can at least be the first customers." (I don't like shopping.) At 9:49 we pulled in front of the frame store. The lights were already on. I could see the sign in the store window announcing their hours as 10-5, but I suggested that maybe if they saw customers waiting outside they might open a few minutes early.

Lisa got out of the car. It was a bitterly cold Canadian morning with a northern winter wind blasting against her as she stepped up to the glass door of the store. Peering inside she could see the shop-keeper. When the woman looked up, Lisa smiled at her. The proprietor smiled back, and then continued with her work. Unperturbed, Lisa began pacing back and forth in front of the store trying to look like a seriously big spender. Whenever the clerk glanced her way, Lisa stopped and gave her a big smile. But to no avail.

Finally Lisa stomped over to the car where I was snugly waiting. Through frozen lips she pleaded, "Don't just *sit* there, *help* me!" I didn't know what to do. But I knew I had better do *something*. So I got out of the car. I'm a fairly big guy and I was wearing a black trench coat and black, mirrored sunglasses. I thought she might show a little more respect to a hulk like me. I opened the trunk of my car to get out the painting and to make it clear we were not just idle window shoppers. But the shopkeeper wasn't even paying attention; she was talking on the phone. So I got back into the car, intending to wait the few remaining minutes before the store opened. Lisa resumed her post.

At 10:03 my wife got in the car and demanded that we leave.

"What do you mean?" I asked. "Surely she'll open up now. It's after 10:00."

"I don't care! Let's go to another frame store. I refuse to do business with these people. Any store that makes customers stand in the bitter cold for ten minutes just because their store hours haven't officially begun is *not* going to get my business. That is a principle with me!"

"Lisa, I know you are a person of principle," I said, "but I'd like to appeal to a *higher* principle." (She probably thought I was going to cite something from the Sermon on the Mount). "That principle is that we have a 50–percent–off coupon at *this* place and we don't have one for any other store."

"I don't care," she said. "I'd rather pay *twice* as much elsewhere than to get it done here for free."

I hated the thought of seeking out another framing shop and squandering what was left of our date. So in desperation I asked, "Well, what happened when you tried the door?"

An awkward silence ensued. Without a word, Lisa got out of the car, walked up to the door, and pulled it wide open. It had been unlocked the entire time. In all her posturing and gesturing Lisa had never actually tried to go inside.

Then we discovered we had been terrorizing the storekeeper. Visibly shaken, she said, "You kept staring at me and smiling at me, *but you would never come in the store.* I didn't know if you were waiting for a written invitation or a red carpet or what." Then she pointed an accusing finger at me. "Then *you* got out of your car. You looked like a mobster! I thought you were going to your trunk to pull out a sawed-off shotgun. I called my sister

God's gift of grace is exactly that—a gift. He doesn't impose it on us.

and told her I had two lunatics outside my store and to be ready to dial 911."

Needless to say, we felt sheepish. And, thinking back, I'm not sure we ever got that discount.

How foolish to spend ten minutes in the freezing cold, peering in at everything we needed but never going in to receive it. We really believed we understood the facts of the situation, but we didn't. And the longer we continued assuming we already knew everything, the less Christlike our attitudes became. God's gift of grace is exactly that—a gift. He doesn't impose it on us. We must receive what He makes freely available.

Grace Assumptions

Whenever I preach or teach on grace I am always surprised at some of the responses I hear. Without fail, longtime Christians and faithful church members will say, "I've heard about grace all my life, but I never fully understood how it's supposed to affect my life."

It is rare to attend a church service without singing about or hearing about grace. However, many churchgoers assume they know all about grace and its wonderful implications. In reality they often have a superficial understanding at best. They can be like Lisa and me, shivering needlessly in the spiritual cold, missing out on all grace could be doing in their lives. So many Christians today are discouraged people standing frustrated outside God's storehouse of grace when the door has been unlocked and everything is inside, prepared and waiting.

I have the privilege of talking to hundreds of Christians as I travel and speak, and I see this enigma all the time. Countless numbers of believers sell themselves short every day because they *think* they know what grace is. But they are missing out on grace's transforming power. The result is needless pain, wasted years, and damaged relationships.

So before we get into the practical ways God's grace can manifest itself through your life, let's take a moment to review what grace is. This may be familiar territory to you, but it provides an important backdrop to what will follow.

Countless numbers of believers think they know what grace is. But they are missing out on grace's transforming power.

A VIEW FROM HEAVEN

Do you ever try to visualize heaven? Although it is an indescribable place, there are enough scriptural whispers to feed the imagination. Picture the magnificent mansions prepared for the saints along the endless glittering golden streets. Imagine the crystal sea. Enter the throne room, the most brilliant vision imaginable. Hear in your mind the exuberant crescendos as the heavenly beings offer their praise to almighty God.

Imagine the celestial celebration when God assembled the earth and created man and woman in His own image. This was the pinnacle of His creation. How beautifully the angelic hosts must have praised God for His amazing work as Creator. Men and women, weak creatures of dust, were designed to enjoy personal fellowship with Holy God, enjoying His love for eternity. God fashioned them with His own hands and gave them the wonderful, joyful gift of life. Even the heavenly hosts could never aspire to such intimacy with God.

Then a horrific tragedy occurred with cosmic repercussions. God's cherished creation chose to rebel against Him. They foolishly assumed they could become gods themselves, that they could rule their own destiny apart from their Creator. They rejected eternal life and embraced certain death. The evil that entered into them immediately separated them from Holy God. Now humanity's dismal future would be marked by pain, suffering, wickedness, and death. They had no hope. They could not go back. Incredibly, despite all they had lost, Adam and Eve and their descendants contented themselves with their lives of sin and death and did not seek to return to the intimate divine fellowship they had lost.

Imagine the scene as word spread across the heavenly city that God was going to restore His fallen creatures. The archangel Michael, commander of the Lord's armies, stood prepared to annihilate the insolent human rebels. Imagine the reaction in heaven when it was revealed the Son of God would be sent to bear the punishment for sinful humanity, to carry upon Himself the full penalty for their sin. This plan must have seemed incomprehensible to the angelic host because God could instantly create more creatures who would obey Him. Why would almighty God humiliate Himself by seeking to restore His rebellious, ungrateful creation?

God's Response

Yet the Creator's response dramatically set Him apart from His creatures. God's nature is perfect. His love is unfailing. Even when His holiness calls for judgment over evil, He welcomes home the prodigal. His love compels Him to show mercy. His grace motivates Him to shower people with undeserved blessings. To this day grace desires to do a work in people's lives. Grace is a gift no one deserves. Grace recognizes people's sin, anger, rebellion, and foolishness but looks beyond all of these to see what these people can become. God's holiness demanded atonement for our sin. God's grace sent His only Son to pay the enormous price for our pride and selfishness (Romans 5:8).

Grace recognizes people's sin, anger, rebellion, and foolishness but looks beyond all of these to see what these people can become.

Heaven's host must have been horrified to witness the sinless Son of God born into poverty in a filthy cattle stall. Surely the peoples of the earth would commence international festivities and rejoicing at the promised Messiah's coming. But for the vaunted Roman Empire, it was business as usual. The Jewish King Herod even attempted to assassinate God's Son.

Once Jesus' public ministry began, heaven's angels may have assumed His divinity would be obvious to all who listened to Him speak or witnessed His miracles. And it *was* apparent to some. Yet many were offended by Him. Some refused to accept any relationship with God in which God set the terms. Eventually sin did its work in dark hearts, and God's own creation conspired against His Son. Evil enticed them to crucify their Messiah on a despicable cross, the method used to execute the most notorious criminals. How heaven must have cringed in horror. The archangel Michael must have longed to mobilize legions of angelic warriors to rescue the precious Son of God. How did Michael remain at his post while cruel humans spit in Jesus' face, beat Him, mocked Him, and killed Him?

But God did not restrain those who brutalized His beloved Son. The punishment for every sin committed by every man and woman, even the trespasses of those carrying out the crucifixion, fell on Christ. At humanity's darkest moment, God's grace shone brightest. God took the most heinous act ever perpetrated and transformed it into His greatest gift (2 Corinthians 5:21). To even begin to grasp the power of God's grace and to become grace-givers ourselves, we need to clarify what grace is and what it is not.

GRACE: WHAT IT IS NOT

Some people view grace as tolerance of anything people do. If a man betrays his wife and abandons his children to pursue an adulterous relationship, we should not judge him because we, too, are sinners. We must show him grace. Some equate grace with weakness. They think showing grace to an enemy or to someone who has offended them is to become a doormat to their oppressors. Some people assume grace refuses to confront sin or to say hard things. Others view grace as something that occurs at the point of salvation, but they have no concept of how it continues its transforming work throughout a believer's life.

Grace is none of the above. It is not a blanket tolerance; it is not a display of weakness; it does not avoid speaking the truth even when it's difficult; and it is not a onetime event. Grace does not ignore sin. Grace recognizes the full ugliness of sin, yet it offers undeserved pardon and blessing.

GRACE: WHAT IT IS

Most Christians have a basic understanding of grace as the undeserved favor or mercy of God toward us. We know we have been saved by grace (Ephesians 2:8). But after salvation, many professing believers have little or no idea how grace impacts their daily lives. Grace is not a onetime gift from God. Because Christians continue to struggle with sin until the day they see Jesus face to face, we need God's grace every day of our lives. He continually supplies grace to His people in countless practical ways. Moreover—and this is where so many of us miss the point—He expects us to be channels of His grace to others.

We are not called to just bathe in grace; we are called to shower it upon others.

We are not called to just bathe in grace; we are called to shower it upon others. Grace has not been fully experienced until it is fully expressed to others. The deeper our understanding of grace, the more we see the necessity of making it the fabric of our Christian life.

The New Testament word *grace* comes from the Greek word *charis*. This word was used by secular Greeks to convey at least three meanings:

First, it could signify a thing that brought pleasure to someone or something that won favor. A delightful meal or a beautiful poem could please people or bring *charis*. Second, *charis* could describe a person in a powerful position showing mercy or favor to someone of inferior rank. When a king chose to act in a kindly manner toward his citizens or when ancient gods were said to bless people, they were demonstrating *charis*. Finally, grace could denote gratitude. To express thanks to someone was to show them *charis*.

Grace appears some 150 times in the New Testament, and the many references clearly show grace's rich and multifaceted nature. Jesus came to earth "full of grace and truth" (John 1:14). While Jesus was the complete incarnation of God's truth and righteousness, He also fully embodied God's love toward those He came to save. The writer of Hebrews described God's throne as the "throne of grace," a place where believers could approach the Lord with confidence (Hebrews 4:16).

The Bible's most zealous proponent of grace was the apostle Paul. He was so enamored with grace he always began and ended his New Testament letters with reference to it. Paul knew God had forgiven his sins, not because of Paul's good works, but by God's grace (Ephesians 2:8–9). Paul realized he was the chief of sinners, and everything God had done for him was a divine expression of grace (1 Corinthians 15:10). For Paul, grace was more than theology; it was the motivating force of his entire life. God's grace moved Him to show kindness to those totally undeserving of it.

Let me outline some truths about grace as we prepare to delve into the amazing realities of grace that apply to your life:

- Grace is a gift of kindness given to someone who does not deserve it.
- Grace is not reciprocal. It goes one way.
- Grace is costly. Someone has to pay the price for grace.
- Grace looks at what people can become and seeks to help them reach their potential. Grace does not condemn those who have not yet arrived.
- Grace focuses on solutions, not problems.
- Grace leads to action.
- Grace is what motivates God to relate to us moment by moment with perfect love. God looks at us through eyes of grace. If He didn't, we would have no hope.
- Grace is the lubricant that eases friction in any relationship.
- Grace expects the best but offers freedom to fail.
- Grace celebrates success and does not keep score of wrongs.

THE POWER OF GOD'S GRACE

Grace is foundational to everything God does in our lives. The apostle Paul's life epitomizes God's grace at work. What was Saul of Tarsus like before he discovered God's grace? Not a nice guy. He was "breathing threats and murder" (Acts 9:1). Saul's entire outlook on life was tainted with thoughts of persecuting and killing Christians. He belonged to the strictest sect of his religion; he was "a Pharisee, the son of a Pharisee" (Acts 23:6). He surpassed his colleagues in zeal for the strict traditions of his religion (Galatians 1:14). He was arrogant, self-righteous, enormously ambitious, and totally committed to his cause. When Saul encountered people who disagreed with him, he threw them in prison, or sent them to a worse fate. He had no tolerance for those who were different or weak.

Grace is foundational to everything God does in our lives.

Then the grace of God stopped him in his tracks and turned his life completely around. All his efforts, studies, and rigorous self-discipline suddenly appeared worthless to him (Philippians 3:4–7). Now instead of propagating hatred, he became a passionate proponent of love (1 Corinthians 13). No longer proud of his accomplishments, he now boasted in his weaknesses (2 Corinthians 12:10). The formerly overbearingly self-righteous vigilante now called himself the chief of sinners (1 Timothy 1:15).

What happened? Saul found grace. Or, more accurately, grace found Saul. And the grace of God was so "exceedingly abundant" that Saul's entire life was radically transformed (1 Timothy 1:12–16). The work of grace in Paul's life did not end on that road to Damascus. It started there. In fact, Paul claimed everything he had become was a result of God's grace (1 Corinthians 15:10). He was not just changed on the outside; grace transformed his entire view of life. Did the apostle Paul believe in the doctrine of grace? Absolutely. Had he *experienced* grace? The evidence is incontrovertible.

MARTIN LUTHER

One of history's greatest testimonies to the dynamic power of grace is the life of Martin Luther. Luther grew up in Germany with plans to become a lawyer. He was a brilliant young man and it seemed certain he would earn a comfortable, respectable living, allowing him to care for his parents in their old age. Then a momentous event occurred in 1505. He was caught in a ferocious thunderstorm and a bolt of lightning narrowly missed him. The harrowing experience shook him to the core of his being. He knew he was unprepared to enter eternity and to stand before God in judgment. So he vowed to become a monk. He entered an Augustinian monastery and devoted his life to God's service.

However, even within the hallowed halls of his religious haven, Luther's sinfulness haunted him. He agonized over Romans 1:17, "The just shall live by faith." He knew he was not just. He was terrified to read that God expressed His wrath against all unrighteousness (Romans 1:18). So Luther exerted enormous effort pursuing a righteousness that God might deem acceptable. He refused to indulge in the simplest pleasures. He spent countless hours tediously confessing his every sin. He even abused his body seeking to gain mastery over his sinful flesh. Yet after he did everything humanly possible to attain a sinless life, he remained painfully aware he was still nothing more than a wretched sinner.

Then one day as Luther was studying Romans 1:17, the Holy

Spirit opened his understanding to the truth of that verse: It is not those who are righteous who have faith; rather those who place their faith in Christ's saving work are made righteous. This simple yet utterly profound truth forever changed Luther's life. In response he took action that sparked the Protestant Reformation, through which countless millions of people found freedom in Christ.

It is not those who are righteous who have faith; rather those who place their faith in Christ's saving work are made righteous.

Luther's message was this: Salvation is a gift from a gracious God. No one can earn salvation or do enough to win God's favor; rather, we are to accept God's free gift. Every promise God has made is waiting to be received if we will accept His grace by faith. When a German monk experienced this life-changing reality, the Protestant Reformation exploded across Europe and Christendom was changed forever.

LIVING IN THE OUTER ROOM

My father is the godliest man I know. He is a giant of faith. He is a champion of truth. He has a vast reservoir of scriptural knowledge. But my dear dad would make an excellent absent-minded professor. A couple of years ago, he agreed to adjust his schedule to speak at a conference in Michigan. The host of the event was delighted. He made every effort to accommodate my father and to make his stay as comfortable as possible.

Dad arrived at the conference hotel late in the evening. He had preached in another state earlier that afternoon and then spent the rest of the day traveling to his new venue. Exhausted, he checked into the hotel and retired for the evening.

The next morning, breakfast was available to conference participants. One of the other speakers recognized my dad and knowing
he'd arrived late the previous evening, asked how his night had
been. Dad replied that his flights had all gone smoothly. He mentioned, however, that he had not enjoyed a good sleep. Dad noted
that the organizer of the meeting had generously assigned him to
an executive room on the top floor of the hotel. His room was
adorned with a twelve-seat boardroom table, a leather couch and
chairs, and a large window with a panoramic view. "The only problem," said my father, "was that the room had no bed."

Not wanting to sound ungrateful, Dad quickly added that the
couch was a hide-a-bed. He had found some linens in a closet and
made up his bed late that night. But a metal bar running under the
mattress cut into his back, regardless of the way he positioned himself. He tossed and turned all night and hardly slept. "I would
gladly have traded the view and the table for a real bed," my father
said wistfully.

"I just can't believe they would put you in a room without a
bed," his friend said. "Are you sure there was no adjoining room?"

Dad meekly excused himself and hurried back to his room. Then, for the first
time, he carefully surveyed it. There was
the door to the closet. And there was the
door to the bathroom. But where did *that*
door lead? He opened the mystery door to
discover a spacious adjoining bedroom
with a king-sized bed. The covers had been
turned down for him by the hotel staff. On the table was a fruit
basket, compliments of the conference host. Everything he had
longed for was on the other side of the door all along. But my dog-

*There is a storeroom of grace
available to every believer—
grace that can enrich your life
in every way imaginable.*

tired dad spent the night on an uncomfortable hide-a-bed.

Would it surprise you to discover God has treasures waiting for *you* right next door? He does. There is a storeroom of grace available to every believer—grace that can enrich your life in every way imaginable. Read on and you'll see what I mean.

BY THE GRACE OF GOD

The fear of missing what God intended for him was a compelling motivation in the apostle Paul's life. He had spent the first half of his life in sin and emptiness. Now he was determined to fully embrace God's gift of grace. He said, "But by the grace of God I am what I am, and His grace toward me was not in vain; but I labored more abundantly than they all, yet not I, but the grace of God which was with me" (1 Corinthians 15:10).

Paul dreaded receiving God's grace in vain. To have all God's kind intentions and loving resources freely available to him and then to squander his life in bondage to his sinful past would have been a travesty. So Paul seized God's grace with gusto. He opened up every area of his life to God. He claimed every promise. Surely, no one has enjoyed the full benefits of God's grace any more than Paul did.

What a shame to have God's grace available to free you from anger, and yet to continue daily in bondage to your temper. How tragic to be enslaved to bitterness, unforgiveness, or anxiety when God's grace can banish these joy robbers from your life. In light of God's bountiful grace, to borrow Paul's words, no believer should receive God's grace "in vain." The reality for every Christian should be the realization of God's promises of joy, abundant life, and freedom from sin.

SET FREE

I teach an adult Bible study at my church on Sunday mornings. It's one of my favorite things to do. I enjoy digging into the Scriptures and seeing the lights come on as people suddenly "get it."

We were studying Colossians 3:1–17 one Sunday. Our discussion centered on the truth that God's grace means we are not bound by the sins of our past. There is no failure or weakness or sin that can hold us captive because God in His grace is prepared to set us free. Then we got to verse eight: "But now you yourselves are to put off all these: anger…" I proceeded to make a statement that immediately immersed me into some *very* hot water. I claimed, "If you are a person who gets angry, then you are an angry person." Seems straightforward, but how do you think people responded? Many of them got angry! There was an explosion of comments and rebuttals and rebuttals of rebuttals. I was reminded that *Jesus* became angry. Several explained their difficult life situations by way of justifying their anger. I was told we should not judge those who are more "passionate" or "expressive" than others.

I held my ground, explaining that no matter *what* you are going through or *how* dysfunctional your upbringing had been or *how* much you struggled with issues from your past, God's grace is still sufficient to set you free from anger.

I cannot remember ever teaching a class when I so utterly lost control of the discussion.

Fortunately, I had to leave town that afternoon. When I returned a few days later, I had a lengthy voice message waiting for me from a woman in that Bible study group. She told me she had been extremely upset at what I had said the previous Sunday. She was insulted that I would make it seem so easy to be set free from anger. She had grown up in a home filled with discord and had struggled with anger most of her life. Furthermore, she had a stressful life and her husband held down a pressure-filled job. They had a child with special needs. Yet she felt that under the circumstances she had coped quite well and did not deserve to be included among those who had "anger problems."

She recounted how she had been so agitated after that class she could think of nothing else. Finally, she decided to pray that God would convict me and deliver me from my hard-hearted, judgmental attitude. As she prayed, she sensed God saying to her, "But you *are* an angry person." This devastated her. Deep down she knew God was right. She cried out to God to free her from the anger that had plagued her and her family for years.

God took the anger from this woman and set her free. And when God sets you free, you are free indeed (John 8:36). A dramatic change was immediately obvious. She had joy. She was constantly smiling. She had experienced God's grace. Had she believed in her mind God could deliver people from any sin? Of course she did. She was a Bible-believing Christian. But she did not realize her theology was far from a reality in her own life. That's what grace does. Grace looks beyond a person's misguided attitude and sees the beautiful potential of a life freed from sin's grasp.

Today hundreds of Christian couples believe God's grace can save them from their sins, yet they have no hope for their marriage as they pursue divorce proceedings. Countless believers affirm the doctrine of God's grace, yet they struggle daily, shackled by guilt from their past. Thousands of church members thank God for His forgiveness while they cling to a grudge against someone in their congregation.

The common denominator is not a lack of biblical knowledge; many of these people are church leaders. The problem is the

Grace is not a concept or a doctrine or an event. It is a continual reality to be experienced and shared.

misconception of what grace is. Grace is not a concept or a doctrine or an event. It is a continual reality to be experienced and shared. It should be a way of life. The heartbreaking truth is that, despite the dynamic, life-changing power of God's grace to utterly transform our lives and our relationships, many Christians receive God's grace in vain.

THE EYES OF GRACE

Does it bother you to know God sees *everything* you do? He never sleeps. He is always alert. He is omniscient. He is fully aware of every sin you commit. He knows of shortcomings in your life even you don't see. You would think that would be a negative experience for God as He constantly observes your failures. Yet God has a unique way of viewing us. He looks at us through eyes of grace. That doesn't mean He glosses over our transgressions or ignores our sin. Jesus came in grace *and* truth (John 1:14). But God does not focus on what *is* but what *could* be. Grace is not fixated on the past but looks toward the future.

Recall that God came to a senior citizen named Abram, who was ninety-nine and still childless. God said, "Let's go ahead and change your name so it better reflects what you *will* be like. Let's call you 'Abraham' meaning, 'father of a multitude,' since that is what you will be one day" (Genesis 17:1–5).

Remember Gideon? His people were so oppressed by the Midianites he had to thresh his grain in a winepress (Judges 6:11). Why? Gideon was hiding in fear for his life because he was withholding food from his oppressors. How did the angel of the Lord address him? "The LORD is with you, *you mighty man of valor!*" (Judges 6:12). Was Gideon a mighty man of valor? Obviously not yet. But he would be. And that's how God saw him. Both Abraham and Gideon would one day be listed in the roll call of the heroes of the faith (Hebrews 11:8–9, 17–18, 32), along with other saints whose lives were transformed by God's grace. Rahab was a harlot when God invited her to join His people. When God's grace had worked in her life, she became an honored role model of faith (Hebrews 11:31) and a member of the Messiah's lineage (Matthew 1:5).

What about the disciple Simon? What name did Jesus give him? Peter (the rock). Was he a rock at the time? We all know the answer to that. Would he become a rock? Yes. In fact he would be foundational in the Christian church, a man whose legacy has blessed generations for over two thousand years (Galatians 2:9; Revelation 21:14).

As these examples and dozens more like them recorded in the Bible show, becoming all God wants for us takes time and lots of grace. Salvation does not mean automatic perfection. Every day God applies His grace to our lives so all that His grace began at our salvation will one day be completed. God never gives up on us. He knows what we can become. That's why our sins and setbacks do not stop His outpouring of grace. He intends to perfect what He began (Philippians 1:6).

After knowing all we do about God's grace, and after enjoying the immeasurable benefits of His love toward us, how should we respond? Does it make sense for us to take in so much and not want to share what we have been given with others? If we truly understand the riches we're receiving, we'll eagerly look for ways to share the wealth.

How do we show grace to others? We look at them through the same grace lens God does. When we consider ourselves, our spouses, our kids, our parents, friends or fellow believers, we know no one has arrived yet. But that is no reason to despair or to give up. God is at work. Just as God continues to apply His grace to people's lives each day, so we must view the work of grace as a process. That means we don't show grace only for a while or in spurts or mete it out as deserved. We open our lives up to become a conduit of God's grace.

CHALLENGE

Here is the challenge. Ask yourself, Do I really understand all that God's grace means for my life? Or have I received it in vain?

Do I really understand all that God's grace means for my life? Or have I received it in vain?

Are you joyful? Are you thankful to God for giving you what you haven't earned? Or are you living your life below the level God intends for you? And finally, are you a sponge or a channel? Do you soak in God's goodness to the saturation point, or have you opened your life up to pour out God's loving grace upon others?

For until you give it away, you'll never fully grasp the reality of God's grace.

3

GRACE: BRINGING LIFE TO RELATIONSHIPS

AVE YOU EVER ASKED GOD to make you a person of grace? How might God answer such a prayer? I serve as president of a theological seminary in Canada. Because we are a small school, we have the opportunity to work with students to develop their spiritual lives and characters as well as their academics. They are wonderful men and women, most of whom come to us from a rich background of service to God. But some call for an extra measure of grace. Occasionally I have new students after their first few weeks on campus come to see me with a litany of concerns and complaints. They offer critiques of the classes, the professors, and the local churches. They point out the many shortcomings of our staff and of my administration.

My initial instinct is to defend myself and to debunk as many of their erroneous observations as possible. Of course that is not always the gracious response. God has taught me several things through these encounters:

First, God dearly loves every student. To be a person of grace, I need to love each one, too.

Second, they have not arrived yet. But then neither have I.

Third, God brings our students to us for a reason. Perhaps He wants me to show them grace in such a way that they move closer toward becoming the people God wants them to be.

It is extremely freeing to remind myself that these encounters are not about me. The important thing is what God is doing in the lives of our students. When I seek to be God's messenger of grace, He gives me the joy of participating in His miraculous work. I have seen God take these disillusioned people and transform them into powerful instruments of His grace. Usually they are bright, creative individuals whose attitudes are actually the manifestation of their eagerness to make a difference in God's kingdom. They are frustrated with having so much to do and yet feel powerless "just being a student." In fact, God has used many of them to become great encouragers to other students and churches. A number of them have returned to thank me for the patience I demonstrated to them during their "early" years. When I see what God is doing in their lives, I am so glad He gave me the grace to be gracious.

When I seek to be God's messenger of grace, He gives me the joy of participating in His miraculous work.

Every encounter I have with someone is an opportunity to impart life-giving words. I can crush a spirit if I'm not careful. To encourage someone is to speak courage into them. To discourage someone is to take away their courage. There are words that give life and words that bring death. Showing grace is all about choosing the former over the latter.

SPEAKING LIFE WORDS

Ephesians 4:29 gives a stirring, convicting directive: "Let no corrupt word proceed out of your mouth, but what is good for necessary edification, that it may impart grace to the hearers."

This is a familiar verse to many of us, yet for years I didn't totally understand it. Let's break it down and I'll show you what I mean.

"LET"—Every word I say is a choice I make. I can't blame anyone else for my words. I decide what I will say and I will be accountable for every word I speak (Matthew 12:33–37), so I'd better choose my words carefully.

"NO"—Is there any excuse acceptable to God for unwholesome words coming out of my mouth? What if I have a bad day? Or perhaps I'm an emotional, expressive person. Maybe someone else spoke harshly to me first. Actually, no means no. God makes *no* allowance for His people to speak unkindly toward anyone. That's pretty clear.

"CORRUPT"—This word means "rotten, unwholesome, putrid." It can be used to describe garbage. You know this type of language. When it's spoken the hearers feel as if they were doused with acid rain or sewage. Corrupt words leave you feeling defiled and disgusted. They suck the life out of you. There are plenty of words like this in the English language. They have no place in a Christian's vocabulary.

"**WORD**"—Words hold power. With a word God created the universe. With a word Jesus raised the dead. With a word hopeless people are encouraged. Likewise, with a word hopes are dashed. Words have the potential to produce great joy or enormous harm. James warned, "No man can tame the tongue. It is an unruly evil, full of deadly poison" (James 3:8).

"**PROCEED**"—In ancient times people believed that vocalizing thoughts gave their words power. Thus, voicing a blessing or a curse caused that oath to become a reality. Their thinking was merely superstition, but they were right about words being powerful. Spoken words do not sit stagnant; they flow toward others, washing them in kindness or drowning them in mire.

"**OUT OF YOUR MOUTH**"—These are the words that concern us—the ones coming out of our own mouth. If we worried more about *our* words and less about what *others* say, imagine the impact on our relationships (Psalm 141:3).

"**BUT**"—This small but important word denotes a contrast. We don't have to accept that our words will inevitably or accidentally hurt others. There *is* an alternative. We can guard our tongue.

"**GOOD**"—This word encompasses what is beautiful and pleasant. Good words are like fresh air to a weary soul (Proverbs 12:18). They bring life to the heart and energize the spirit.

"**NECESSARY**"—*Everyone* needs to be built up and encouraged. We live in a corrupt, darkened, sin-filled world. Life has a way of knocking us down and sapping our strength. Words of kindness and grace are not a luxury; they are a necessity.

"**EDIFICATION**"—Edification implies building up, strengthening, or making better. Words can do that. Good words bolster people facing the impossible or enduring the unthinkable. Kind words bring healing to deeply wounded souls. Corrupt words tear down. Good words build up.

I have always understood this passage up to this point. It cautioned me to watch my language, and to refrain from gossip, criticism, and other inappropriate language. I generally considered this verse in negative terms, warning me what not to say. But one day the last part of the verse caught my attention: "*That your words may impart* grace *to the hearers.*"

I had always assumed grace was something *God* gave. My obligation was to avoid careless language while God was the One who imparted grace. This verse gives another perspective. We are to be meticulous with our words because they are a potential source of grace—God's grace— to people who desperately need it.

Words of kindness and grace are not a luxury; they are a necessity.

Our words have the power to give life to others. What an incredible privilege. What an awesome opportunity. What a frightening thought! Every day we are surrounded by people who need to be built up. The world has battered them down. People have deceived them. Life has confused them. But we have the words of life that can encourage them and make them stronger. Words of grace, from God, through us will give them hope and refresh their souls. Every encounter with another human being is an opportunity for us to share "life" words or "death" words.

DEATH WORDS

Why do I call corrupt words death words? Because they sap the life out of the hearer and their devastating effect can linger for decades. In chapter 4 we'll discuss words of grace within the family setting, but let me relate an example here to illustrate the life-robbing effects of our words.

I once knew a pastor who was growing increasingly frustrated with his teenager. His son was regularly in trouble and struggling at school. The boy attended church but he made it painfully obvious he did not want to be there. This pastor was embarrassed by his son's behavior.

One Sunday their relationship reached a boiling point. The boy was sitting in the back pew, chatting with his friends during the sermon. Even worse, he was wearing his baseball cap. This blatant display of irreverence pushed his father beyond his tolerance level. From the pulpit, the pastor interrupted his message to angrily chastise his son, demanding he stop talking and remove his cap at once. Five hundred people witnessed life ebbing out of that boy. He eventually quit attending church altogether.

LASTING EFFECTS

Many adults still carry emotional scars because of the harsh words someone once said to them. Successful, respected men and women tearfully recall the demeaning words their parents spewed on them in moments of frustration. Though the words were spoken decades earlier, the pain is as acute as if the altercation took place that morning. And parents aren't the only guilty parties. Any person who has authority over others should understand the power of words and be diligently cautious in what they say.

Fungus Brain

I was not the most brilliant student ever to grace the halls of a high school. But my parents always encouraged me to pursue the necessary classes and credits so I could go on to college. I needed to study a language to be eligible for university so I enrolled in French. I had the misfortune of landing three years running in the class of the school's toughest French teacher. All she spoke in class was French. Once I began falling behind, I could not catch up.

Many adults still carry emotional scars because of the harsh words someone once said to them.

One day Madame Meanie asked me a question in French. I had no clue what she said. I took a shot in the dark and offered a feeble response. My teacher bristled in front of the entire class and in English (for my benefit) she declared, "Richard Blackaby, you have a *fungus* for a brain!" My dreams of an Ivy League scholarship plummeted to earth. That was the end of my language study.

Those words haunted me throughout my senior year of high school. I assumed I wasn't very bright. Perhaps I was fooling myself even thinking of university. I went to see the guidance counselor, and as I kept disparaging my academic ability, he stopped me mid-sentence. He showed me my grades and said, "Richard, I don't know why you're talking like this. Your grades are perfectly good enough to get you into university." I had thought of myself as a fungus brain because that's what my teacher said I was.

LIFE WORDS

Life is full of irony. Years later I felt God leading me to enter a PhD program. The requirements were stringent, but the greatest hurdle was that I needed two years of German and one year of *French*. To make matters worse, no grade under a B was acceptable. Even though I had done well in graduate school, the specter of taking French again after all those years loomed like an ogre before me. My mind raced back to that day in high school where my brainpower was dissected before the entire class. I had since acquired two degrees and was now seven years older, yet I felt as if I were back in high school again. I dreaded those language classes.

Fortunately this time I had a teacher who gave words of grace. Bob talked to me as if he assumed I could do it. He celebrated every success and took opportunities to affirm me. On one day I passed both my German and French final exams (perhaps not with flying colors but I *did* pass). The power of words…we have all felt their effect for better or for worse.

GRACE AND ENCHILADAS

God has been working me over in this matter of giving grace to people. It doesn't come naturally. Two years ago I felt convicted I was not the person of grace I ought to be. So I prayed a dangerous prayer: "Lord, help me become a person of grace." Of course we know how God answers prayers like that. He rolls out ample opportunities for practice.

I was scheduled to speak at a conference in the Southwest. I had spent all morning on a plane and finally arrived at an airport over an hour away from the conference center. My host suggested we grab something to eat at an airport diner before setting out on the highway. We chose a Mexican restaurant (my favorite food) and I eagerly ordered the enchilada platter. I hadn't eaten all day and it was mid-afternoon.

I prayed a dangerous prayer: "Lord, help me become a person of grace."

When the server arrived with our meals, I prepared to indulge myself. She set my friend's plate down in front of him and then, as she leaned across the table to set my heavy platter in front of me, she dropped it. There was a loud *crash*, and enchilada sauce, refried beans, and Spanish rice flew *everywhere*. Hot enchiladas landed in my lap. I had only two pairs of pants to wear for the week and one of them had just been smothered in Mexican food. I would be pulling rice out of the cuffs of my pants all the way to the meeting place. My suitcases and my computer bag were both dripping with tomato sauce. It was oozing its way through the zippers on my luggage.

The first thoughts racing through my mind were not life words. But as irritated as I was, the Holy Spirit whispered into my soul, "So you want to be a person of grace? Here's your chance." As I looked at the waitress frantically cleaning up her mess, the Spirit let me see her as God must have viewed her. She was an older woman, distraught and humiliated by what she had done. The clatter of the mishap had attracted the attention of everyone in the restaurant.

The rest of the waitresses (all much younger) seemed disgusted with their older colleague. None of them offered to help. One of them walked by and tossed a wet cloth at the befuddled woman who was desperately muttering apologies and trying to scoop up the food that had exploded everywhere. In that brief moment I believe God let me sense what He sees in these situations.

This woman was at an age when she should have been home gardening or playing with her grandkids. Instead she was doing manual labor with a group of coworkers who were one-third her age. She was probably earning minimum wage. The plate load she was carrying was too heavy for her (and obviously more than I should have eaten anyway). I wondered what family and financial pressures drove her to this difficult job.

I realized I had done something divine, and it felt really good.

As I watched her scrape food off the floor, I knew what grace would do. I got out of my chair, squatted down beside her, and started to help her. She kept apologizing, assuring me she could manage. I could see the embarrassment in her eyes, so I smiled and told her that at my home I was often on cleanup duty, and I didn't mind helping now. As I looked into her face, I saw relief and appreciation.

That encounter did something to me, too. I realized I had done something divine, and it felt really good. (For months afterward, every time I set my luggage out for my next trip, my dog Chevy would start licking my suitcase. He likes Mexican food, too.)

God's Word on Our Words

Scripture has much to say about the words we speak and their power to produce good or to wreak devastation. Consider a few examples:

Proverbs 15:1–2: "A soft answer turns away wrath, but a harsh word stirs up anger. The tongue of the wise uses knowledge rightly, but the mouth of fools pours forth foolishness."

Proverbs 22:11: "He who loves purity of heart and has grace on his lips, the king will be his friend."

Proverbs 25:11: "A word fitly spoken is like apples of gold in settings of silver."

Proverbs 25:15: "A gentle tongue breaks a bone."

Ecclesiastes 10:12: "The words of a wise man's mouth are gracious, but the lips of a fool shall swallow him up."

Matthew 12:34–35: "'For out of the abundance of the heart the mouth speaks. A good man out of the good treasure of his heart brings forth good things, and an evil man out of the evil treasure brings forth evil things.'"

Matthew 12:36: "'But I say to you that for every idle word men may speak, they will give account of it in the day of judgment.'"

Colossians 4:6: "Let your speech always be with grace, seasoned with salt, that you may know how you ought to answer each one."

GRACE WORDS FOR RELATIONSHIPS

Human relationships depend on communication. The words we speak dramatically affect the quality of the relationships we enjoy. Have you ever been blessed with a friend whose words were gifts to your soul? I have—in fact I've had several. When you are going through a crisis, who is it you'd like to have call you on the phone? With the advent of caller ID, we have the ability to screen our calls.

God can transform anyone into a person of grace, if that person is willing.

At times when I've had a hard day and the phone rings, I see who's calling and my heart is lifted just knowing who it is. Some people know how to use their words to uplift your spirit. At other times I'll see the name and think, "Just when I thought things couldn't get any worse…"

It is difficult for some people to use their words to bless others. Perhaps they suffer deep insecurities. They subconsciously fear that by lifting up another they will somehow lower themselves. Others are too needy or self-centered to take time and effort to encourage others. They are so hungry for attention themselves it never occurs to them to focus on others. Perhaps the saddest cases are those who have no idea how to verbally share grace. These are often the victims of dysfunctional parenting. They were raised on a diet of criticism and ugly talk, and now they carry on the family tradition by feeding this poison to their families.

But the truth is God can transform *anyone* into a person of grace, if that person is willing. Here are a few principles I have found helpful as I've sought to improve my grace-giving abilities:

- *Focus on the positive, not the negative.* There is almost always something positive you could point out if you really try. If you have to address something negative, begin and end with a positive word. Ask God to help you see people as He does.

- *Don't waste time talking about things that can't be changed.* For example, if the heartbroken mother of a rebellious teenager shares her grief with you, it is pointless to tell her what she should have done when her child was ten. That only adds to her guilt. It certainly doesn't lighten her load (Galatians 6:2).

- *Make it a habit to ask questions of the other person* instead of steering the conversation back to you and what you have done or what you are going through. You already know about you. Learn something new and interesting about someone else (Proverbs 18:2).

- *Constantly evaluate* whether your conversations are building people up or tearing them down (Proverbs 12:18).

- *Choose to talk about things that matter.* Too many of our conversations are meaningless or downright drivel. Remember the scriptural warning to "shun profane and idle babblings, for they will increase to more ungodliness" (2 Timothy 2:16).

- *Don't worry about conversations where each speaker gets equal time.* Show an interest in someone else and watch that person's whole countenance brighten (Philippians 2:3-4).

- *There are no more powerful words* than "I forgive you" or "I am sorry" or "I was wrong." Try saying them, regularly.

- *Consider withholding a comment.* Sometimes the gracious response is not to say anything when you disagree with someone but to allow the Holy Spirit to speak to the person instead.

A DIVINE PURPOSE

Relationships all have a purpose. God brings people across our path for a reason, and it's our privilege to respond. If He has brought someone into your life or led you to a particular church family, He has not necessarily put you there to seek a blessing, but so He can use you to bless those people.

I remember one Sunday hearing a young man speak during a college-oriented service. I was struck by his poise and sincerity as he recounted his spiritual pilgrimage. After the service I sought him out to compliment him on a fine message. I asked him if he had considered whether God might be calling him into full-time Christian ministry. He seemed taken aback and thanked me for the encouragement. The next day he called me and asked if he could meet with me. Over lunch, he shared that God had indeed been calling him into Christian ministry, but it had scared him to death. He had prayed that if God wanted him to do so, He would make it crystal clear to him. Right after that I had approached him with my question. That young man is currently in seminary and loving it. He is serving the Lord in his church, and the fruits of his ministry are everywhere.

That encounter made me wonder how many other times God had something for me to communicate to someone but I was oblivious to His activity.

I don't share this event to sound as if I am always attentive when God wants me to speak to others. In fact, that encounter made me wonder how many other times God had something for me to communicate to someone but I was oblivious to His activity. That experience showed me how thrilling it is to be a part of God's work of grace in people's lives.

My father, Henry, is keenly watchful for such opportunities.

One day in a worship service Dad noticed a young man on his knees at the front of the church during a corporate prayer time. Dad joined him, put his arm around him, and began praying out loud that the young man would trust the Lord and obey all God was telling him. The young man looked to see who was praying with him and exclaimed, "It's you!" Then he explained: He was in law school preparing to become an attorney, but he had sensed God calling him to go to seminary instead. He knew this was a major decision and that going into the ministry would greatly disappoint his parents. In that worship service he asked God to make His will unmistakably clear. Suddenly the author of *Experiencing God: Knowing and Doing the Will of God* had his arm around him praying he would follow through with what God had told him.

When I was a pastor, I used to pray through the church directory for every person in our congregation. One Monday I came to the name of a young man who had recently married. As I prayed for him, I knew he and his wife faced significant challenges. Their finances were tight and her health was fragile. I felt impressed to write him a note. I assured him of God's love and that God was in control of their lives—so they could trust Him. I signed it "Your pastor" and dropped it in the mail.

On Wednesday the phone in my office rang. "How did you know?" a voice said. Puzzled, I asked, "Who is this, and how did I know what?" It was the man I had sent the note to on Monday. He responded, "How did you know that today I would lose my job?"

He had gone to work that day to discover a drop in government funding had caused his corporation to be downsized and his job to be lost. He was handed his final paycheck and sent home. As he returned to his apartment he was bewildered. He didn't know how he would pay that month's rent. His wife was too ill to work. He felt as though he had nowhere to turn. But there in his mailbox was my letter. He knew the note was not really from me, but from God. He knew he didn't have to fear the future because God was in control. What a difference a simple card can make.

God uses His people as messengers to deliver His words of grace to those in need.

Let me reiterate: For every time I have gotten it right with God's prompting, I wonder how many times I have missed His invitation. God uses His people as messengers to deliver His words of grace to those in need. So many times I knew God wanted me to say something to someone and when I did, I saw the reason God led me to do it. My prayer has been, "Lord, if there are people around me who need a word of grace, would you use me to deliver it to them?"

EXUDING GRACE

When I was in university our church would have a "Secret Valentine" week every February. People put their names in a hat, and they were paired with a "secret valentine" for the week. The idea was to send them anonymous notes or drop off presents without them guessing your identity. It was a lot of fun. Being a young, eligible university student, I hoped to draw the name of a pretty, single female. Instead my valentine was a frail, elderly widow by the name of Mrs. Abriel. She was not anything like what I had hoped for. I had probably not spoken three words to her. We had nothing in common. But I tried to be a good sport. I sent her some things during the week, and at the end of the week, I went with my dad, who was the pastor, to visit her in her rest home.

Mrs. Abriel exuded grace. She was one of the most humble,

kind, thoughtful people I ever knew. I had gone to encourage a lonely widow, but I came away with the blessing. I was so enamored with her I offered to pick her up for church on Sunday mornings, and so developed a wonderful friendship between a university student and an elderly widow. When I would pick her up, she was always ready and waiting by the door. She was always grateful. She would pepper me with questions about my week and my challenges at school. When I asked about her week, she would gently laugh and say, "Oh, nothing happened with me." And then she would focus on me again. She would ask me how she could pray for me, and I knew she did so all during the week.

One weekend I had to be out of town and I forgot to arrange for someone else to pick her up on Sunday. She waited by the door that morning for some time before realizing no one was coming to take her to church. The next Sunday, I apologized profusely for the inconsiderate way I had treated her. She would hear none of it. She said she knew how busy I was with so many things to remember. Besides, she said, she had enjoyed a special time with God that day alone in her room and she was grateful for that. She gave me grace.

One day my father told me Mrs. Abriel had suffered a stroke and was in critical condition in the hospital's intensive care unit. He was going to see her and wondered if I wanted to go along. I was terrified. I had never been around someone who was dying, and I didn't know what I would say. But I had to go.

She was extremely feeble when we arrived. Yet I still remember her gentle smile when she saw me approach her bedside. Then she kindly scolded me and told me I was far too busy to take time out of my day to come all the way to the hospital to visit her. But she was grateful, and she thanked me for my kindness to her. Only an hour or two after our visit, Mrs. Abriel slipped into eternity. To this day I still feel the impact of the consistent grace she showed me. She was truly a person of grace. I have prayed that I could one day be that kind of person, too.

A WORLD OF LIES

The Bible calls Satan the "father of lies" (John 8:44). He captivates people by his deceptions. Satan tells people they are worthless, they are unimportant, they are inferior, and their sins are unforgivable. People are craving words of truth and grace. The prophet Isaiah proclaimed, "How beautiful upon the mountains are the feet of him who brings good news, who proclaims peace, who brings glad tidings of good things" (Isaiah 52:7). There is no way to measure the joy of sharing God's grace with the fearful, the discouraged, and the lonely. We all know from experience the joy of being on the receiving end of such a blessing.

There is no way to measure the joy of sharing God's grace with the fearful, the discouraged, and the lonely.

Why don't you ask God to use you this week to deliver a message of grace to someone who really needs one?

4

GRACE: BRINGING LIFE
TO YOUR FAMILY

ONE SUNDAY I was the guest speaker at a church. Afterward an associate pastor took me for lunch and shared with me his recent pilgrimage. His seventeen-year-old son had been drifting from the Lord and delving into hard, secular music. The teen, who played the guitar, joined a local rock band that performed in bars and nightclubs on weekends. Because the young musician was often out until the early morning hours, he rarely made it to church anymore. The heartbroken pastor pleaded with his son not to throw his life away by rejecting everything good and decent he had been taught. His arguments fell on deaf ears. The son embraced his immoral lifestyle with increasing fervor.

One Sunday morning the situation hit a heart-wrenching low. The son confessed that his girlfriend was pregnant and they were considering an abortion. This news pushed the father over the edge. He blew up at his son, spewing the pent-up fury that had been brewing from months of disappointment and frustration. He labeled his son a disgrace to God and to the family, and threatened to throw him out of the house until he came to his senses. Then the pastor charged out the door.

Anger and embarrassment flooded over him as he drove to church for the Sunday service. How could his son be so blinded to the destruction he was causing himself and others? How would they explain his son's situation to the congregation?

As he approached the church building, he saw the cross and was reminded of Christ's death for people's sins. The Holy Spirit nudged his heart, "What do you think the cross was for? Was it not for sinners like your son?" The pastor pulled his car over and wept. It smote him that at the very time his son was most desperate for a loving dad, he was pushing him away. If ever this confused young man needed grace, it was now. Despite his many years of speaking, teaching, and singing about grace, in this critical family moment the pastor realized he had no idea how to show it. But he knew who did. "Lord, help me know how to show grace to my son!" he tearfully entreated the Father.

That's when God began a miracle in the family. My pastor friend decided to attend his son's performances at local bars whenever he could. The next weekend, as he stood outside the door of the tavern where his son was performing, he was suddenly seized by panic. He glanced up and down the street to make sure no one from his congregation saw him entering such an establishment. But if his choice was between impressing his church members and making an impression on his son, he would choose his son. He found a table close to the stage and ordered what he hoped was a noticeably nonalcoholic looking beverage. This straight-laced teetotaler may as well have worn a placard that said, "I DON'T BELONG HERE."

When the band came on stage, the boy was shocked to see his father in the audience. At the intermission, he quickly made his way to his father.

"What are you doing here, Dad?" he asked. "You hate this music and you hate this kind of place."

"You're right, son," his dad said, "but I love *you*, and I think you need me right now. So I won't embarrass you. You don't even have to acknowledge me. I'm just going to sit here and pray that you experience God's very best in everything you do."

But if his choice was between impressing his church members and making an impression on his son, he would choose his son.

This father, though he had been in Christian ministry all his adult life, was learning a whole new dimension of practical grace. "Do you know what?" the pastor asked me. "After I went to see my son in that bar two months ago, he has been in church with his girlfriend every Sunday since!"

Grace is an undeserved gift. It uplifts the soul. It gives life. It builds up. If there was one place we should be generous with grace, it is within our home. God designed the family to nourish healthy self-images. The home is where people first experience love. Home is where people should find security and forgiveness. This has indeed been the experience for many.

But the words *home* and *grace* don't always blend. For countless others the most painful moments of their lives occurred at home. How tragic. God's grace can make the home an oasis of peace and joy. Yet innumerable homes resemble war zones rather than safe havens. Families attack and wound one another because they don't understand grace and they don't know how to apply it. There are several areas in the family where grace can do its miraculous work.

GRACE IN MARRIAGE

When I was in university and dating Lisa, I lived on a student's budget, so I had a meager wardrobe. I wore outdated pants, old tee shirts, and a ratty corduroy jacket. My hair was a sorry excuse for an Afro. My teenage kids recently saw a picture of me as a college student standing next to their mom. They exclaimed, "Mom, what were you thinking! Were you *that* desperate?" Teenagers have a way of keeping you humble.

I remember the week after Lisa and I became engaged. There was a party at my house, and at one point I realized Lisa was missing. I finally discovered her in my basement bedroom. She had a large garbage bag and she was throwing away most of my clothes. I was horrified!

"Lisa, what are you doing?" I gasped.

"Now that we're getting married, you're going to have to take better care of your appearance," she said.

"But aren't you marrying me for who I am?" I said.

"No, I'm marrying you for who I'm going to make you." And she has been true to her word these twenty-plus years.

We still laugh about that incident, but Lisa was committing the rest of her life to help me become the man God wants me to be. She has laid her life down many times so I could follow God's will. I believe that is what Ephesians 5:25–26 commands husbands to do as well: "Husbands, love your wives, just as Christ also loved the church and gave Himself for her, that He might sanctify and cleanse her with the washing of water by the word."

How was Christ able to leave heaven's glory and submit Himself to brutal torture for our sins? Grace. Jesus didn't have to die for us. We did nothing to earn His sacrifice. There is no way we can make it up to Him. But God looked at our sinful condition and He knew how His grace could transform us. He willingly gave us the gift of salvation if we would receive it.

Likewise Paul said your spouse has not yet become the total person God intends. But that's okay. God has granted you the privilege of walking with your lifelong companion, showing grace and helping your partner achieve everything God has planned. That's the intention of marital grace. Grace builds up your spouse, strengthens your marriage, and helps you both become like Christ.

God has granted you the privilege of walking with your lifelong companion, showing grace and helping your partner achieve everything God has planned.

My father did a wise thing when he became engaged to my mother. He asked her to share with him the commitments and promises she had made to God in her youth. He pledged that when they were married he would spend the rest of his life helping her keep every promise she had made to God. What a wonderful thing: two people walking together through life, selflessly striving daily to help each other become like Jesus. That is God's plan for marriage.

MARITAL GRACELESSNESS

You're familiar with the first couple, Adam and Eve. What happened as soon as they sinned? Their relationship took a nosedive (Genesis 3:12). I wonder how often the subject came up in later conversations?

Adam: "Eve, if you hadn't given me that fruit to eat, we wouldn't be in this mess."

Eve: "Well, no one made you eat it. And besides, where were you when that snake came around? You're never here when I need you!"

Ever since sin entered human relationships, couples have struggled to treat each other with forgiveness and grace.

Last year I had a man ask me to meet with him and his wife because his marriage was under duress. That evening I sat in their lovely home. The exquisite furnishings had been collected from around the world. Their nanny put their children to bed. The couple served me delicious refreshments and everything seemed pleasant, until they started telling me about their marriage.

The husband began recounting the difficulties they were experiencing. His wife would periodically interject facts he had failed to mention. According to *him,* he had tried to provide for his family and to build a godly home, but his wife had begun to reject her faith and to neglect her family. According to *her,* her husband did not care about her; he was totally consumed by his job. *He* was the one neglecting the family as she was expected to take care of the household duties. She was not free to have a life of her own. As she told her side, he would frequently interrupt to "set the record straight."

Here were two professing Christians who could not speak civilly to one another. That evening we uncovered a multitude of hurts and misconceptions that were compounded every time they opened their mouths. I witnessed their marriage suffer repeated verbal deathblows and realized their relationship could not withstand much more. From my vantage point every problem they presented was fixable, if they would choose to forgive and to work on their marriage instead of continually justifying their own perspectives. Healing was possible, but virtually every word they spoke inflicted another wound. This couple did not understand grace. They had both been saved by grace, but they had no idea how to give grace to one another.

Grace doesn't insist on *being* right. It seeks to *make* things right. Grace doesn't demand to be heard. It strives to listen and to understand. Grace doesn't claim its rights. It voluntarily lays them aside. Grace doesn't look for wrongs. It seeks out what is right. The problems in this marriage are addressed head-on in Ephesians 4:29: "Let no corrupt word proceed out of your mouth, but what is good for necessary edification, that it may impart grace to the hearers."

The church is plagued with graceless marriages, characterized by words of death rather than words of grace.

Why is the divorce rate among Christian couples comparable to that of nonbelievers? Allow me to boldly answer my own question. It is because Christians think they understand grace, but they really don't. I know that may sound simplistic. Even now your mind may be racing to come up with exceptions and extraneous circumstances. But the fact is the church is plagued with graceless marriages, characterized by words of death rather than words of grace.

I'll never forget meeting a pastor's wife who had been in the ministry for four decades. She sadly acknowledged to me, "There is no joy in our home." I wondered what she and her husband understood grace to be. Grace brings life. Grace refreshes the soul. Grace makes things better. A home cannot be filled with grace and be void of joy. That's not possible.

GRACE AND AN AIRLINE TICKET

I love my wife intensely, but she and I are polar opposites. I am driven and task oriented. Lisa lives for today and loves a party. I am a saver. To her, "delayed gratification" is the time it takes to drive to the mall. I am a thinker. She is a feeler. I have warm feet; she has ice cubes. Marriages like ours don't work unless grace abounds.

Several years ago I received an unbelievable opportunity. I was invited to participate in a "Revival Tour." Our group would travel throughout Great Britain visiting noteworthy sites of church history and especially locations famous for revival and spiritual awakening. I was delighted. My degree is in church history. At that time I was preparing to teach a seminary class on the history of revivals. What a perfect time to see firsthand the places I'd studied for years.

The only problem was that I'd have to be away for two-and-a-half weeks during the summer. Our children were very young, and I knew it would be hard on Lisa to remain behind with the kids. However, she knew how much this trip meant to me and what a great opportunity it was. She urged me to do it, so I eagerly signed up and bought my ticket.

Lisa's health was not good at that time. She was secretly dreading my absence. She didn't know how she could manage without me. She had encouraged me to go because she wanted what was best for me, but her apprehension increased daily. Finally one day she broke down and tearfully confessed that she did not want me to go.

As a cognitive person, this struck me as irrational. I could understand her wanting me to stay, but she should have told me this before I bought a $1,200 nonrefundable ticket. The thought of wasting that kind of money chewed away at me. I thought, *You should have told me sooner. It's too late now. Maybe next time you'll tell me the truth when I ask!*

Feelings of disappointment, frustration, and confusion swirled around in my mind. But then something happened that I'll always remember. The Spirit of God stopped me cold and nudged my heart: "Be a man of grace."

As long as I considered the expense and embarrassment I would face in canceling my trip, I was frustrated. But as I looked at my sweet wife, I saw something else. This was the woman who had worked like a Trojan, walking with me through seven years of seminary and four years as a pastor's wife. She had often been a "single parent" to our three kids as the demands of school and ministry occupied me. She was struggling now, and I realized there was something far more important happening here than my getting to go on a trip. This was one of those "for better or for worse" times. It was not a time to demand my rights or to insist on what was fair or reasonable. This was a time to lay my life down for my wife.

It's amazing how showing grace to someone has a way of softening your heart.

It's amazing how showing grace to someone has a way of softening your heart. The moment I gave up that trip for Lisa, my love for her flourished, and so did our marriage.

I have kept that airline ticket. I don't show it to Lisa; it is a reminder to me of what is really important. Scripture commands husbands to lay down their lives for their wives. I had to forfeit only money. Every time I see that ticket it reminds me there is no price tag on the value of my relationship to my wife. I would pay *any* price to preserve what Lisa and I have.

This story has an interesting sequel. Two years ago my parents took all their kids and grandchildren to England for two weeks for a family reunion. I was able to travel to London after all, but this time with my wife and kids. Lisa and I went jogging each morning along the Thames River past the Tower of London and across London Bridge. It was a glorious trip we will always remember, together. And I got to visit all kinds of old churches where dead saints are buried, while Lisa explored Harrod's famous department store.

Lisa's health has improved significantly, and I have gone on a number of international speaking trips while she has held down the fort at home. She regularly lays *her* life down for me. But I am so grateful that at a vulnerable time in her life, God stepped in and helped me practice grace. Showing grace to your spouse takes on many forms. Here are a few reminders of things we all know but maybe forget to practice.

To show grace:

- You speak words intended to build her up, not to bring her down.
- You focus on his needs rather than your own.
- You freely forgive.
- You swallow your pride and say "I'm sorry" and "I was wrong."
- You seek opportunities to bless her with your words and actions.
- You live out your marriage with the goal of "no regrets."
- You don't keep score or worry about what is fair.
- You lay your life down for your spouse just as Christ laid His life down for you.
- You read 1 Corinthians 13 *regularly.* It's all there so you don't forget.

GRACE TO YOUR CHILDREN

God intends for our childhood home to be the place we form our first impressions about Him. It should be where our parents model God's character for us. If we want to know what our heavenly Father is like, we should get an idea by watching our parents. To understand forgiveness, we should see it lived out before us. The unconditional love and acceptance taught in the Bible should be a regular experience in our families as we grow up. Will Rogers once quipped, "So live that you wouldn't mind selling the family parrot to the town gossip." Sadly, this ideal is often missing in Christian homes.

Unconditional love and acceptance should be a regular experience in our families as we grow up.

GRACE AND BLUE HAIR

Last year our church was having a pictorial directory made of the congregation. I had the brilliant idea of getting a good family picture and then using it in promotional pieces for the seminary. I could already imagine sending Christmas cards to all the seminary alumni and donors with a picture of my attractive family and me. Unfortunately I forgot to inform my family of this plan.

On the day of our appointment, my gorgeous wife emerged from the bedroom prepared to take the camera by storm. My thirteen-year-old daughter, Carrie, made her entrance looking fabulous as always. Next came sixteen-year-old Daniel, his chin length hair mostly covered by a knit hat (we call them toques). He looked like he was about to knock off a convenience store. "That's OK," I thought. "We'll remove the cap before the picture."

But then my eighteen-year-old son, Mike, appeared. For reasons I will never understand, Mike had decided that afternoon it would be "cool" to spike his hair and dye it fluorescent blue. I couldn't believe my eyes. Words of death began jockeying for position in my head. The shocked look on my face warned my wife that an unpleasant moment was brewing. She quickly took me aside and admonished me that before I said anything I would regret, I should recall that Mike has always been a good kid. Although he liked dyeing his hair unusual colors, when it came to important stuff, he had always made me proud. He wanted to be an individual and to be cool. He had done nothing that a few shampooings or a good head shave couldn't cure. So I let it go.

How foolish it would have been to speak harsh words that Mike would remember for years over something that would not last two months. God looks at what is important, and I doubt hair color is on His priority list. However, my son is a great source of joy to me. He enjoys his church, he has his own walk with God, he is a young man with high integrity, and he is heading toward Christian ministry. I'm quite sure these things are more important in God's eyes.

Words I've regretted have usually been thoughtless reactions to trivial matters.

I have learned that words I've regretted have usually been thoughtless reactions to trivial matters. How tragic to speak words of death for something so superficial. And to be honest, my frustration was really not with Mike's hair. I was upset that his action had disrupted *my* plans. I have no business speaking to my family members or anyone else when I am angry. Anger never produces grace; love always does. In that unguarded moment, I was in danger of hurting my family, and for something so meaningless (Proverbs 19:11).

(By the way, we did have that picture taken—Daniel looking dashing in the toque, and Mike's beaming smile rivaling the brilliance of his hair.)

GRACE AND SCHOOL

I wish I could say I have always been careful to show grace to my kids, but I have not. At times my self-centeredness has overcome my better judgment, and I have really blown it as a dad.

I remember a time when my schedule was unusually brutal. I was facing some huge challenges at work. I was solving problems all day long. Then one evening Lisa told me Daniel was experiencing severe difficulties at school. He was seeking to live out his Christian faith, but he was facing persecution and bullying. He had come to the end of his rope and he didn't want to go to school anymore.

I wish I could tell you I handled things as a compassionate Christian leader and father ought to, but I didn't. My first thoughts were about me. I couldn't handle one more problem, especially in my own family. My life was so filled with responsibilities at that time I desperately needed everyone in my family to just be happy.

I impatiently headed for my son's room to find out what was wrong. I wanted to quickly solve his problem so I could get back to mine. I recounted with him my own difficult experiences at school and how I had survived it by toughening up and grimly getting through. When he wasn't overly inspired by my pep talk, I grew frustrated. I didn't have time or energy for my son to be unreasonable. We live in a fairly small town, and I knew of no other option but for him to continue attending that school. Yet my son was distraught. I finally announced that he *would* go to school and he *would* make the best of it just as I had many years before.

I was only a few steps from his room when the Holy Spirit began to awaken my conscience. I was ashamed at how I had just acted. My son was going through the worst time in his young life, and when he looked to his father for help, he had not received an ounce of grace.

The Spirit immediately began helping me know what I should do. For one thing, grace would have me truly seek to understand my son. I am a thinker; my son is a feeler. He was so hurt he was saying things that did not sound logical to me. I shouldn't get frustrated because he didn't process circumstances the way I did. Being a feeler had made Daniel a kind, sensitive kid. Being a feeler also meant it was hard for him to keep dealing with the pain he was experiencing at school. And telling my son I survived what he was going through didn't help matters. Survival wasn't the point here. Daniel was "surviving," too.

Grace doesn't worry about inconvenience; grace focuses on what is important.

Grace would seek to empathize with what he was going through. Grace would not preach survival; grace would find a solution. Grace doesn't worry about inconvenience; grace focuses on what is important. Right then Daniel's situation was considerably more pressing than any other problem or deadline I faced. Grace pays the price to make people like Christ. I had tried to get off easy.

As I stood in my bedroom crying out to God, I knew my precious son was in the next room, desperate for a dad who could show him grace. I prayed, "God, if you'll give me another chance, I'll go back in there and try that again." And I did.

Fortunately I have discovered that God, and your kids, will give you grace to try again. That evening launched my son on a unique pilgrimage that continues to this day. He has developed into a wise young man of strong character, one who knows God loves him and who knows his dad loves him, too.

We parents sometimes become frustrated with our kids for still being kids. They have not arrived yet. They can still be immature. They can make unwise choices. But grace patiently takes people from where they are to where God wants them to be. Grace understands that what God began in our kids, He intends to complete (Philippians 1:6). The question for parents is whether we will choose to participate in what God is doing in our children's lives.

I believe our role is to be lifelong cheerleaders for our kids. They live in a difficult world that wants to chew them up and spit them out. They need people who believe in them. They need to know they can always count on mom and dad for support.

A few years ago my nephew was also going through a tough time at school. He was doing his assigned reading and came across the word *advocate*. He asked his mom what it meant. She explained that it referred to someone who was "on your side" or "in your corner." With a deep sigh he said, "That's what *I* need, Mom—an advocate."

Selfishness and good parenting don't mix. I know everyone needs "me" time, and I know it's not healthy to "lose one's identity" during child-rearing years. But let's face it—parenting is a selfless venture. It just isn't right for mom and dad to focus so much on their own needs that they resent the time and attention their kids take. Many parents confess they spend scant time with their children because they have nothing in common or they don't enjoy doing the same things. So they sit in different rooms all evening. The kids play video games and dad watches football.

I'm glad God didn't watch us from heaven and bemoan the fact He had nothing in common with us. God *found* common ground. He took the initiative to communicate with us. If left up to us, we would have remained forever alienated from God. But He saw our weaker condition and, in His grace, He met us at our level to demonstrate His love for us.

Grace motivates parents to listen to the brain-jarring music their kids like and then say, "Wow. That's really something, isn't it?"

My teenage kids often excitedly play for me "the coolest song there is." It usually sounds like every other song they have played for me—a very bad singer shouting at his dog. But they seem to like it. Grace motivates parents to listen to the brain-jarring music their kids like and then say, "Wow. That's really something, isn't it?"

Grace leads parents to wearily get up out of their recliner at the end of a long day to shoot baskets with their kids or to bake cookies with them. Grace doesn't selfishly pursue only our interests or likes. Grace looks for what is really important: a meaningful relationship with the kids God entrusted to our care.

Grace and Garage Doors

Six years ago Lisa and I had a new house built. Neither of us had lived in a new home before. It was pristine. It was spacious. It was expensive! I was worried sick about interest rates, resale value, and depreciation. One evening my wife and I were having coffee in our new living room, when suddenly we heard a loud BANG. I thought a small aircraft had nose-dived into our roof.

I ran outside to discover it was my two boys playing street hockey in the driveway. Mike had fired a blistering slapshot at

Daniel in goal, but he missed the net and hit the garage door instead. Sure enough, I found a large "ping" in my otherwise perfect door.

"Sorry Dad!" they cried out in unison.

"You'd *better* be," I muttered. And then I delivered a moving speech on resale value and on being good stewards of what God gives us. They promised to be more careful.

I had barely sat back down with my coffee when I heard another BANG. This time I scrambled out the door mumbling something about what I was going to do to my boys with their hockey sticks. While surveying Ping #2, I ordered them to pack up their hockey gear and to go find a school playground or a parking lot or a freeway—*anywhere* else to play but in the driveway of my nice new house. They insisted there was nowhere else, and they repeated their vow to be more careful. I would hear none of it.

Triumphantly, I returned to my wife and my cold coffee. Lisa looked at me and said, "I guess we'll have to decide if we're going to live in a home or a museum." That hurt. As she so often is, Lisa was right. Our two teenage sons *liked* being at home. Here I was encouraging them to find somewhere else to hang out. I did some quick calculating and determined that for only a couple hundred dollars, we could eventually replace the door. The boys could get paper routes and each pitch in half. But in the meantime, our kids could build happy memories in their own driveway.

Today, when I give directions to our home, I usually say, "Find the house with the garage door that looks like it suffered a machine-gun barrage, and that's us."

Lisa and I decided to make our house a place of grace, where important things were made important and unimportant things were minimized. Don't misunderstand me to mean our kids trash the place. It's just that a garage door is a lot easier to repair than the feelings of a teenager who doesn't feel welcome in his own home.

Last year I came home from a trip while my wife and kids were out of town. I knew the house would be empty when I arrived. Yet I was so used to seeing the boys in the driveway shooting hockey pucks or basketballs that I instinctively looked for them as I rounded the corner.

A garage door is a lot easier to repair than the feelings of a teenager who doesn't feel welcome in his own home.

The driveway was empty. I pulled in and gazed upon a thousand pockmarks (or rather puck marks) on my battered garage door. In that moment it hit me: Before long those kids wouldn't be in that driveway anymore. They would be married with their own families and my lovely house could then become a museum filled with memories of what once was.

It was a sobering moment. I realized a day was coming when I would notice the marks on the garage door and remember the mighty hockey games that were played, or the scuff marks on the ceiling where a pool cue had experienced lift off, or the scratches on the windowsill where our dog Chevy used to put his paws as he watched for the kids to come home, and I would dearly miss those days.

I'm not sure I'll ever replace that garage door. Some memories are priceless.

GIVING GRACE TO PARENTS

While not everyone reading this book may have a spouse or kids, most of us have had to learn how to relate to our parents. Scripture is clear we are to honor our mother and father (Exodus 20:12;

Deuteronomy 5:16; Ephesians 6:2). In fact, this is the only one of the Ten Commandments that comes with a promise of blessing if we do it. The question is often asked, "But what if my parents aren't honorable? What if they hurt or betrayed me?" The Bible doesn't qualify which parents are deserving of honor. It just says to honor them.

The Bible doesn't qualify which parents are deserving of honor. It just says to honor them.

As parents get older, sometimes they can be frustrating. They get set in their ways. They can disagree with what we are doing or how we are rearing our kids. We may remember times our parents disappointed us or failed to be there for us. Everyone has these memories.

There is no question some parents have inflicted great pain on their children. I would never minimize the suffering people have endured at the hands of dysfunctional parents. Yet I also know that to truly be a person of grace, you can't pick and choose those to whom you give it to. The more I come to see myself as God sees me, and I realize the magnitude of God's grace toward me every day, the easier it is to see my parents through eyes of grace.

GRACE AND CROOKED TEETH

I was blessed to grow up in a warm, loving home. But it was not perfect. My mother has never been shy about telling her children what she thought. At times I have disagreed with her opinion. But through the years (especially after having my own children), I have come to view my mom with the same grace she has shown to me all my life.

Not long ago Mom spoke at a ladies' dessert fellowship at our seminary. She told the ladies that when I was a teenager, I had not worn my retainer as I should have after my braces were removed. That's why my teeth are so crooked today, she explained, despite all the money she and my father had paid the orthodontist. Well, the women had a good chuckle as they listened to the seminary president's mother chastising him in his absence. How embarrassing! I didn't smile for weeks.

Yet even as I heard about how my mom made me the brunt of laughter, I knew I could respond to her only with grace. After all, I didn't have to think very hard to recall many sacrificial things she had done for me.

When I was a teenager I used to go hunting at 4:30 in the morning. Mom would get up early enough to make me homemade biscuits for breakfast. I used to play hockey games that went past midnight, and my mother would faithfully be in the stands, cheering on her son. To this day I know that if I am facing any challenge in my life, she would move mountains to help me. So I would be a fool to focus on a little thing when she has proven over and over again that she loves me.

You can look for faults in anyone and find them, if that's where you choose to focus.

Remember John from chapter 1? Somewhere along the way he forgot about all his parents had done for him that was *right,* and he began to fixate on what they had done *wrong.* You can look for faults in anyone and find them, if that's where you choose to focus. Showing grace doesn't mean you're blind to another's shortcomings. Some parents have committed horrendous sins against their children, and grace does not condone that or minimize the resulting pain. But grace searches out those things that are good, those things that bring hope. Our heavenly Father is fully aware of every flaw in us, yet He also knows what we can become. And He never gives up until He sees His love do its transforming work in us (Philippians 1:6).

GRACE AND A CHANGE OF PLANS

I know a young couple who both became Christians and, soon afterward, they began to sense God calling them into Christian ministry. They decided to quit their jobs, sell their home, and move several hundred miles away to attend seminary. Everything went pretty smoothly until they informed the wife's parents of their plans. Her dad had a conniption. Though he claimed to trust God, he saw no reason why his son-in-law should quit a lucrative job and cart his daughter and grandchildren to a distant school to train for a career that would be filled with hardships and struggles. As the couple persisted in their plans, the man grew angrier. Finally he refused to acknowledge his son-in-law in any way. He would not speak to him or respond to any communication from him. Even when his son-in-law tried to hug him goodbye, he stood rigid and unmoved.

Their first year at seminary was painful. They grieved over the acrimonious parting. They smarted from the unkind words that had been spoken. Yet they chose to respond with grace. They regularly wrote letters home and told the parents how God was miraculously providing for them and answering their prayers.

The following summer the couple returned home for a visit. As they pulled into the driveway, the father-in-law approached them in tears. He confessed that despite claiming to be a Christian, he now realized he did not have the kind of personal walk with God that his daughter and son-in-law had. He now understood why they had obeyed God's call, and he declared he wanted to know God as they knew Him. Not long after, the son-in-law had the privilege of praying with this broken man to receive Christ as his Savior.

Words and actions of grace have a powerful effect, even on a hardened heart.

CONCLUSION

A family that lives by grace is a powerful tool in God's hands. God taught Abraham grace and then promised him his descendents would bless the families of the earth (Genesis 12:3).

Some of you reading this book did not grow up in a home of grace. But now God is calling you to establish such a home with your family. If you have not been gracious toward your parents, ask God to show you how. Keep in mind that grace isn't grace if it is deserved. Consider your relationship with your spouse. Have your words been life words or death words? Have you chosen to focus on the positive and on what could be? Have you regularly demonstrated grace through forgiveness? Would you want God to show grace to you in the same manner you have given it to your spouse? Finally, would your children describe you as a person of grace? Do your words bless your kids? Is your home a sanctuary of grace? If not, would you like it to be?

Ask God what you need to do to make your home a place where grace flourishes. Don't ever give up or settle for less than God's best for you and your family.

5

GRACE: SHARING LIFE WITH OTHER BELIEVERS

SEVERAL SUMMERS AGO I was invited to speak to a group of university students at a beautiful lakeside retreat center in British Columbia. I took my family along so they could enjoy the time with me. Our three kids soon linked up with other children who had accompanied their parents.

One day the children invited all the parents to a church service they were conducting at an open-air amphitheater by the lake. Each child had a role. One made announcements; another led the singing; two children sang special music. Then they announced they were collecting an offering. We parents, playing along, placed stones and leaves in the makeshift offering plate. But the collection taker sternly rebuked us—we should give our offering "as unto the Lord." She reminded us God was not mocked; we would reap what we sowed. So we all dug deeper into our pockets.

After the sermon, an altar call was extended. When none of the adults walked the aisle in repentance, we were told the singing would continue until *everyone* had been made right with the Lord. My wife, Lisa, finally went forward and the singing concluded. But then to Lisa's dismay, the kids began dragging her to the lake to baptize her. "Wait!" she shouted. "I've already *been* baptized. I'm rededicating!"

The following day, as Lisa walked past the amphitheater, she could hear the kids' voices. She smiled as she remembered the delightful church service of the previous day, but as she drew closer, she was disturbed to hear arguing and angry words. She hurried over to stop them. "Kids! Kids, don't argue! Yesterday you all played so well together. What happened?" They all smiled and one of them said, "Oh, it's OK. Our church is having a business meeting." (Out of the mouth of babes…)

If there is one sure place to experience grace, it ought to be in church.

If there is one sure place to experience grace, it ought to be in church. After all, church people have experienced grace firsthand through their own salvation. They hear grace preached from the pulpit and taught in their Bible studies. They often sing about grace and refer to it in public prayers. Some churches even bear the name "Grace." Yet sadly, grace is often in short supply in the very place it ought to be abundant.

GRACE SHORTFALLS

I remember when my father was called as pastor of a dwindling, discouraged congregation. He took a substantial pay cut at a much larger church and moved thousands of miles to shepherd this small flock. The small parsonage overflowed with our family of seven as well as numerous visitors. We often hosted summer missionaries and visiting speakers. Our home had only one small bathroom.

After some time, a motion was made at a church business meeting to install a second bathroom in the basement where we four boys shared two bedrooms. The wealthiest man in the church spoke up. He considered it wasteful to spend money on a second bathroom when the church was already strapped financially. Finally, he reluctantly agreed the church should provide basic bathroom fixtures, but he saw no reason to build walls around the bathroom as only boys were living in the basement. When other members insisted the church also pay to construct walls, the man indignantly left the meeting.

As a young boy I was astonished that someone with enough personal wealth to build ten bathrooms was so stingy with the church's resources. I'll never forget the kind way my father related to that man afterward, despite his angry exit. I saw the ugliness of gracelessness and the beauty of grace in the same incident.

I wish that incident was an anomaly, but unfortunately it is symptomatic of a widespread problem in the church. Consider the following scenarios and see if any resonate with your experience:

- The worship leader introduces a new music style and is inundated with disparaging e-mails Monday morning.
- A new Christian relapses into sin, so church members shun her until she finally stops attending.
- The church votes to undertake a mission project, and those families who disagree with the venture withhold their tithes from the church.
- The building and grounds committee chooses a contractor to renovate the facilities, and a member who unsuccessfully bid for the job unleashes his fury at the next business meeting.

- The pastor's wife is derided for joining an adult Bible study rather than teaching a children's Sunday school class.
- The new pastor is frequently reminded of the "Camelot" days when his predecessor more ably led the flock.
- The pastor makes widespread changes in the church without consulting anyone. When members question his actions, the pastor has them removed from leadership positions in the church.

Why are Christians so unkind to one another? It is because we lose sight of our own daily need for grace. We begin taking our salvation for granted. We forget the reality that we are sinners, saved by grace. A heart that is oblivious to God's continuous gift of grace soon becomes calloused toward others.

God's people are a forgetful lot. Skimming through the books of Genesis and Exodus will easily prove that point. Perhaps that's why Paul always began and ended his letters to churches by mentioning grace. He urged his protégé, Timothy, to "be strong in the grace that is in Christ Jesus" (2 Timothy 2:1). The writer of Hebrews warned, "Pursue peace with all people, and holiness, without which no one will see the Lord: looking carefully lest anyone fall short of the grace of God" (Hebrews 12:14–15).

REVIEWING GRACE

Let's take a moment to review what grace looks like:

- Grace builds up; it doesn't tear down.
- Grace gives what is undeserved.

- Grace is costly.
- Grace gives without expecting anything in return.
- Grace thinks of others, not self.
- Grace focuses on the important, not the trivial.
- Grace looks at what could be, rather than fixating on what is or is not.
- Grace helps people become more like Christ.
- Grace doesn't condemn or give up on people.
- Grace emphasizes mercy, not justice.

These are the traits that ought to characterize the bride of Christ. When people become Christians and join a church, it doesn't mean they no longer need grace. It's just the opposite. The church attracts people who recognize their desperate need for grace.

GRACE AND TAX COLLECTORS

Jesus was perfectly holy and sinless. He never compromised truth or excused sin, yet sinners were constantly drawn to Him. Righteousness is attractive when it is combined with grace.

One day Jesus was enjoying a meal in a house with several tax collectors and people of questionable moral character (Matthew 9:9–13). In the Middle East, allowing someone to share a meal with you meant you were opening up your life and friendship to that person. The Pharisees were scandalized by Jesus' behavior. How could He be so loving and welcoming to people

We must look past people's current spiritual condition to see what God's grace can make them.

who were clearly sinners? They just didn't get it. Jesus' response was, "Those who are well have no need of a physician, but those who are sick."

That is our cue for how to "do church." Like Christ, we must look past people's current spiritual condition to see what God's grace can make them. And we should hope and pray the same grace is applied to us. One of those dining with Christ was Matthew, who would become an apostle and the author of the Gospel bearing his name. By spending time with society's outcasts and various other "unacceptable" people, Jesus was investing His life in what He knew was important. That's what grace does.

GRACE AND SENIOR CITIZENS

A few years ago I went to a church to conduct a series of meetings. The church enjoyed a wide diversity of people in its congregation. Saturday evenings they had a contemporary worship service that attracted mostly the younger crowd. There were three Sunday morning services, all with different worship styles. But for this week, everyone from all four services would meet together each evening, from the rock generation to the pipe organ devotees and everyone in between. I was curious to see how it would all work out.

The first evening service went well. It was advertised as "Hymn Night." There was a senior adult choir, and we sang old favorites such as "The Old Rugged Cross" and "How Great Thou Art." Everyone seemed to enjoy the service. But the next night was going to be the challenge. A youth worship team was on deck to play for that service.

I arrived at the church early that evening. Before I entered the auditorium, I could already hear the drums and electric guitars as the musicians tuned up for the evening. I wondered how the large segment of senior citizens would respond, if indeed any came. As I entered the sanctuary I was surprised to discover the older set already filling the pews at the back of the auditorium.

I approached a row full of older men and women and asked them what they were doing at church so early.

"Oh, we wanted to make sure we could get the seats farthest away from the music," they said.

"That loud music hurts our old ears," one woman explained.

"Well, I'm so glad you came out tonight anyway," I said.

"Oh, we wouldn't miss it," they responded. "Our grandkids *love* this music."

Another enthusiastically added, "And a lot of young people are finding Jesus and being baptized. It's *very* exciting!"

As I looked across the rows filled with seniors, I saw dear saints who loved God, loved their church, and loved the young people God was sending them.

"But how do you handle the loud music?" I asked.

Two women smiled at each other and then said, "We have a secret weapon." They both dug into their purses and produced earplugs. "Can't hear a thing!"

Sure enough, when the time came for me to speak, I could see the whole group prying out their earplugs so they could hear the sermon.

These wonderful people understood what was important. The salvation of young people was more important than getting to sing their favorite music. They rejoiced because the younger generation enjoyed coming to church. They "got it" that grace is about giving. These senior folks were undoubtedly the ones who covered most of the church expenses. Many of them had served the congregation for decades, maybe even as founding members. They could have demanded their "rights." But instead they went out of their way to bless their young people.

The teenagers obviously admired these senior adults and the older people experienced the joy of seeing young adults love and serve Christ. *That's* what a church of grace looks like.

GRACE AND A NEW BELIEVER

I was the brand-new pastor of my very first church. One of the first people I met was a young woman named Vivian. She was not a believer, but her five-year-old boy attended the church playschool, so she started bringing him to church on Sundays. Vivian had not experienced an easy life. She had lived with a man, the father of her son, for nine years. He was unfaithful to her and verbally abusive.

Through a ladies' Bible study, she soon became a Christian. She was one of the first people I baptized. As she regularly studied the Bible, the Holy Spirit spoke to her about changes she needed to make. Now that she had encountered grace, there was much in her life that needed sorting out. She soon became convicted that she should not be living with her boyfriend. She moved into a guest room in their basement and told her boyfriend they needed to marry. He agreed, bought her a diamond ring, and then stalled until it became obvious he had no intention of marriage. Finally she found affordable housing and moved into it with her son. Cut off from the financial resources she had counted on for years, she sought a job for the first time in a decade. People in our church helped her and her son. One church member hired her at his company.

Over the next several years the church ministered grace to her. And she blossomed as a believer, showing incredible maturity for one so new in the faith. Her son and my two boys became great friends. In fact all three were baptized on the same day. During difficult times church members prayed for her and encouraged her. Years later Vivian told me she had uncovered a box in her closet filled with letters of encouragement church members had written her over those difficult early years.

She remained on friendly terms with her son's father. Some time later he discovered he had cancer. He was fearful of the prognosis and turned to Vivian for support. She married him and allowed their son to experience living with both his mom and dad together. Vivian faithfully nursed and cared for her husband, loving him for the remainder of his life. Before he died, he accepted Christ as his Savior.

Today her son is a leader in the church, and she is a faithful member and encourager of others. Vivian had been scarred and defiled by the world, yet because she experienced God's grace through her church, she in turn became a beautiful person of grace.

That's what churches do. They share truth and grace with hurting people and watch the Holy Spirit transform those people into saints.

CHURCH PEOPLE NEED GRACE

Often it's easier to extend grace to non-Christians than to fellow believers. We assume people in our church shouldn't need grace as much. They should "know better." They shouldn't continue to struggle with selfishness or sin. We expect them to always do the right thing. But grace recognizes that God's transforming work in our lives (called sanctification in the Bible) is a process. We aren't perfect, nor should we expect perfection from fellow church members.

I grew up playing Ping-Pong with my brothers. Recently we inherited a Ping-Pong table, and I am teaching my daughter, Carrie, to play. At first she seldom connected with the ball. So I yelled at her and got angry, right? Of course not. I taught her the tricks my dad taught me. She loves to play and is improving daily. Her goal is to beat her dad one day. Every time she misses a ball or forgets what I taught her, I don't slam down my paddle and look for a better opponent. I give her another chance. I celebrate the shots she does make, rather than focusing on what she misses. Guess what? She's getting pretty good. Soon I may have to cheat or fake an injury.

We aren't perfect, nor should we expect perfection from fellow church members.

GRACE AND EASTER DINNER

When I went to my first church to serve as pastor, I assumed my flock would adore me and appreciate all the time and sacrifice I gave them. Not all of them did. One evening I was leading a church council meeting. We had just experienced a wonderful series of meetings at the church. Several had come to a saving knowledge of Christ and many others were blessed and encouraged. I prepared for a pleasant gathering as we reviewed God's activity the previous week.

Instead, one lady began to criticize me for what she thought I had not done. She wouldn't let it go at a simple reprimand; she went on and on itemizing the many ways she thought I had messed up. I was dumbfounded. I felt as if I had been spewed on for thirty minutes. As soon as I got home, the phone began ringing as others from the meeting apologized for the woman's behavior and pleaded with me not to resign.

Several days later, on the morning of Good Friday, I received a phone call from the same woman. This time she criticized me for something else. And a simple apology was not enough; she wanted her pound of flesh.

When I finally hung up, I was angry. I knew I wasn't a perfect pastor, but I had worked hard and whatever oversights I had committed did not merit these tongue lashings. To make matters worse, I discovered this woman had cornered my wife in the church hallway and yelled at her. Now *that* chapped my hide.

That Friday morning I opened my Bible to review my Easter Sunday message. I read about the Passion, how people cruelly tortured and crucified Jesus. In those quiet moments the Holy Spirit drew my attention to the love and grace Jesus demonstrated even to His tormenters. Knowing people were blinded by their sin, He cried out, "Father, forgive them, for they do not know what they do." I realized I could not get up on Easter Sunday and preach about the wonderful news of God's grace unless I was first willing to demonstrate Easter grace to this woman.

I shared my thoughts with Lisa. To my surprise she said, "Why don't we invite her and her family over for Easter dinner?" I wasn't so sure about that. My parents were visiting from out of town, and I had been looking forward to a special family time. Now my wife was suggesting we invite Attila the Hun-ess to repast with us.

But I knew Lisa was right. I lost the coin toss and called the woman. When she recognized my voice, I could sense her defenses going up, bracing herself for a counterattack. Instead, I told her our plans for Easter. I said Lisa and I had talked about whom we wanted to join us and we had both thought of her family. Would they be able to make it? She was stunned. "What can I bring?" she stammered. "Nothing but your appetites," I replied.

That Sunday we experienced a wonderful Easter service. I spoke about God's grace that motivated Him to send His Son even when people were cruelly mocking Him and rejecting Him. I sensed the power and beauty of God's grace being exercised in my life even as I spoke.

The woman and her family came for dinner, and we all thoroughly enjoyed ourselves. As she grew to trust me, she eventually shared some deep hurts she had experienced in the past at church and confessed she had misdirected her anger toward me. She ultimately became a friend and a wonderful support to my family and me.

Everyone needs grace. We have all grown up in a sinful, graceless world. People have been hurt and disappointed over and over. Many still bear scars from abuse or betrayal. As a pastor, I could not get frustrated with people when they acted like people. It was for folks like them (and me) God designed the church.

A DANGEROUS MISCONCEPTION

A misguided presumption among churches is that showing grace means a blanket tolerance and acceptance regardless of what someone does. Often churches welcome back into full fellowship people who grievously sinned, even though these people remain unrepentant or even defiant. At times churches so misunderstand what grace entails, church members feel guilty even mentioning the person's sin. "After all," they say, "who are we to judge?" Pseudo grace avoids dealing with sin and instead focuses on being "loving."

But showing genuine grace never involves condoning sin. Grace never compromises truth or righteousness. Jesus forgave the woman caught in adultery but He also commanded her to "sin no more" (John 8:11). Jesus had lunch with the most

Showing genuine grace never involves condoning sin.

notorious sinner in Jericho, but right after dessert, Zacchaeus was making amends for his sins by repaying fourfold all those he had wronged (Luke 19:1–10). Genuine grace always draws people toward Christ and His righteousness. Pseudo grace tolerates sin and muzzles those who would speak against it. A loving, graceful response to sin sometimes means caring enough to say the hard thing that may help people understand the consequences of their sin (Proverbs 27:5–6).

Take a moment to evaluate whether you are showing people genuine grace or pseudo grace. If your response to sinners is not encouraging them to turn from their sin toward God, you may be showing them tolerance, but not grace. Grace moves people toward where God wants them to be. Grace also focuses on what is important. If a person is persisting in sin, that individual's repentance before God is far more important than immediate restoration into the Christian community.

A COMMON OVERSIGHT

Jesus claimed the world would recognize His genuine disciples because of their love for one another (John 13:35). Loving one another involves showing grace. Although 1 Corinthians 13 is often used in weddings, it was written to the church at Corinth whose members were acting proud and un-Christlike toward each other. To paraphrase that passage:

True love:

Does not grow frustrated and give up on those who are less mature.

Does not get jealous.

Doesn't seek recognition or steal the limelight.

Subdues pride, refusing to capitulate to hurt feelings.

Does not act unkindly.

Keeps loving regardless of the other person's response.

Doesn't retaliate because of injury.

Always assumes the best in people.

Never compromises with sin.

Keeps hoping.

Remains faithful.

Jesus said this kind of love should characterize the church. Yet we Christians often shift our focus from loving others to the pressing matters at hand. We value our tasks and results more than our fellow believers. We defend our opinions and comfort rather than seeking the best for those God has placed around us.

PRESS DELETE

I am a school administrator. I deal with problems daily, big and small. Several years ago I was working with a large denominational bureaucracy. Some top leaders were making unilateral decisions that would harm our seminary, and I was frustrated. We had worked hard and God had blessed our school with significant progress. This agency's decision could greatly set us back.

I sat down at my computer and pulled up the e-mail address of my contact person. He had not made the questionable decisions, but I wanted to vent on someone connected to the organization. I hurriedly typed out my grievances, including several rather acidic accusations. I skimmed over the caustic paragraph and prepared to hit "send." Something within me made me hesitate. I am generally easygoing and try to act professionally, but I was annoyed and I thought someone should know it. So I hit "send." Even as the computer processed my command, I knew I had made a mistake. If I could have crawled into my computer and retrieved that message, I would have. But it was too late.

I worried that my hasty message would further harm my school. What if this person chose to play hardball with me? There was little I could do. The recipient of my message, I realized, had always been kind and helpful to us. I knew he would be as frustrated with his organization's plans as I was. He did not deserve my diatribe. Because of my frustration with a process, I had attacked a person. I decided I needed to make things right with him face to face.

Two weeks later we both attended a meeting in another city. As the first session ended, I hurried over and apologized to him for my message. He brushed it off and said he understood how frustrated I must have been. He never mentioned it again. He showed me grace.

Several personal resolutions grew out of that incident. First, I resolved to never forget that people are more important than programs. Activities come and go. People are eternal. Grace always sides with the person. Second, I realized that because I am a recovering sinner, my first instinct is often sinful. I have to be careful about my initial response to people. It isn't always Christlike. In fact, with regard to e-mails I now operate by this principle: If I hesitate over the "send" button, I need to hit "delete." If the Spirit causes me to waver about what I am about to say, I had better not say it. Instead, I need to ask God to help me communicate only those things I won't regret. The beauty of e-mails, or anything you write, is that you get to review and revise your words before you send them. I try to always ask myself, "Is my message going to build up or tear down the person who receives it?" To be a person of grace, I have to be in the business of bettering people, not battering them.

When Christians keep their focus on God and His activity, it is much easier to show grace. When we concentrate on our activities or our own concerns, giving grace becomes a challenge.

You can tell people's focus by the observations they make. Those who gripe about all the young children running about in the church foyer or about how difficult it is to find a place in the church parking lot don't have their focus on God's activity. When people complain they "get nothing" out of the worship service, it shows they misunderstand the purpose of worship. Those who criticize the pastor for never being available to them may demonstrate a misunderstanding of the pastor's role.

People of grace, however, thank God for the little ones at church. They sign up for nursery duty. They park down the street to leave the best spots for visitors. They focus on God, not themselves, in the worship hour. And they offer to help ease the pastor's harried schedule by making a hospital visit or two for him.

Unhappy in the Pew

One day I heard that a couple in my church was unhappy and considering leaving the church. I paid them a visit that evening. They began by mentioning various things about the church that were unsatisfactory. However, as I probed some more I realized their primary concern was that they had no friends in the congregation. No one ever called them or socialized with them. They felt hurt and lonely, so they decided to leave.

They still viewed church in terms of what it did for them, rather than as a means to serve others.

As tactfully as I could, I asked them what *they* had done to befriend others. How many people had they reached out to or invited to their home? Their answer was two blank stares. Although these two were longtime church members, they still viewed church in terms of what it did for them, rather than as a means to serve others. They agreed to start reaching out to others. They soon made friends and were amazed at how the church changed!

GRACE AND A REBATE

A church filled with people who are looking for ways to serve others is a great place to be. My wife loves giving gifts. In fact, I complain that her ability to *give* exceeds my ability to *earn*.

When our church was smaller, she was the financial secretary and issued the year-end tax receipts. One year she noticed that a single mom had faithfully given to the church all year despite having very little income. Lisa was so moved by the woman's faithfulness she placed in an unmarked envelope an amount of money that equaled the woman's yearly contribution and left it in her church mailbox.

That dear woman never learned how it happened, but she knew God cared for her needs and honored her faithfulness. Lisa found such joy in that venture she repeated it the next year, too. (I was never so relieved as when she quit that job and began teaching Sunday school!)

GRACE IS FOR SINNERS

I was blessed to grow up in a church where grace abounded. We had numerous college students in our church, and there were always several romances flourishing. Our church tradition was for couples to announce their engagement at the conclusion of a service. One Sunday a young couple came forward at the altar call. As the congregation awaited the happy announcement, the couple tearfully confessed instead that they had not been pure in their relationship and the young woman was now pregnant. They were heartbroken over the effect their sin would have on their parents and on the church. It was a painful moment for all.

But then our pastor (my father) said, "You have heard their confession and their request to be forgiven. Would those of you who feel led to do so gather around them and pray for them?" The entire congregation left their seats, encircled the couple, prayed for them, and forgave them. In that powerful moment, the church experienced grace and truth.

Grace is for sinners. God demonstrated grace best when He extended the gift of forgiveness and salvation to humanity, none of whom deserved it. To be like Christ, the church needs to be a redemptive community. The church ought to be a safe haven for repentant sinners. Instead it has often been a place of gossip and ridicule. Many transgressing Christians have felt forced to leave the church because they could not face the shame and rebuke they would endure at the hands of their own congregation.

But thankfully there have also been innumerable times when sinners thought there was no place they could be accepted or forgiven, and then they came to a church and were showered with love and grace. We all know stories (I hope) of how people of grace led others into a restored relationship with Christ and His people. Here are a few examples from my experience:

- A husband committed adultery. He repented and was helped by his church to receive counsel. Ultimately he sought and received forgiveness and reconciliation with his wife. They are happily married today.
- A husband struggling with explosive anger finally pushed too far and his family fled for safety. The church helped him be set free from his anger and to be restored with his family.
- A teenage girl became pregnant. Although she was not a Christian and did not attend church, our church held a baby shower for her and several women walked with her throughout the pregnancy.
- A man struggling with alcohol continues to receive food and rides from church members even though he frequently breaks his promises and never repays money he "borrows."
- A man with few social skills is befriended by church people and welcomed into their homes even though he continually says rude, inappropriate things.
- A woman struggling to leave behind her immoral lifestyle is accepted into the church fellowship and given counsel, encouragement, and respect.

- A teenager is in rebellion, using drugs and refusing to attend church. Yet the youth group keeps reaching out to him and finding ways to include him.
- A woman and her daughter both have special needs mentally and physically, but they are trying to live on their own. They are loved, accepted, and included in all aspects of church life and constantly receive gifts and anonymous donations.

The world does not understand grace. Grace is rare in people's experience. It is something God instigates and enables. When God's people truly grasp what grace is, the church becomes irresistible to the world. In an age of hatred, terrorism, and division, the message of grace has never been more necessary. The church has an unprecedented opportunity to provide something the world is sorely in need of.

But Christians have to know what grace is and how to share it. The church, of all places, ought to be a haven of love in a hurting and grace-starved world.

6

GRACE: GIVING LIFE TO UNBELIEVERS

WHILE ATTENDING SEMINARY I worked three years at a psychiatric hospital for teenagers. To accommodate my class schedule, I worked the night shift from 11:00 p.m. until 7:30 a.m. As I arrived at work one night, the staff from the evening shift expressed their condolences to me. I asked who had died. They informed me I was getting a new nurse to oversee my unit. Her name was Bobbie. Bobbie had previously been a charge nurse on day shift, but she had been so unpopular with the orderlies they conspired to have her exiled to the graveyard shift.

Bobbie had suffered a difficult life. Mistreated as a child, she had grown up severely mistrusting everyone. This was evident in her relationships. She had been divorced five times before the age of forty. She had several noticeable nervous habits and wore a permanent scowl. Her lack of tact alienated her from her staff so workers were constantly applying for transfers to other units.

Those under her supervision would sabotage her authority at every opportunity. Any mistake she made was quickly reported to upper management.

Finally hospital administrators had heard enough. They gave her two choices. *Option one:* transfer to the graveyard shift with fewer staff to offend, be placed on three-month probation, and see a psychiatrist once a week. *Option two:* be fired. She chose option one.

As the evening staff (a little too gleefully) filled me in on what awaited me, my heart sank. The night shift was tough enough already.

Bobbie trudged down the hall to the nurse's station, frowning. She acted as though she was serving a sentence (which I guess she was). She looked at my shift partner and me, and she saw two staff people who looked just like the ones who had caused her banishment. She was extremely cool toward us and said little.

I would love her and show her kindness if it killed me.

Visions of tedious nights working for Bobbie loomed like Banquo's ghost before me. I was a full-time doctoral student. I was also working full time trying to pay for school and support a wife and two babies. The last thing I needed was an antagonistic boss, but I resigned myself to my fate. After all, I was training to be a minister. This could be a course in long-suffering. Something in me loves a challenge. Though she had left a trail of angry workers and wounded colleagues behind her, I determined to be the nut she couldn't crack. I would love her and show her kindness if it killed me.

Of course it wasn't easy. It became immediately clear she didn't trust my partner or me. She would check up on us constantly.

Words of encouragement were nonexistent. One night she spewed out something so rude to me I spontaneously burst out laughing. Even she could see the absurdity of her comment, and she began to laugh, too.

I prayed regularly for grace during those long nights. As God helped me view her through His eyes, I saw a lonely, hurting woman. She had failed often in life and in relationships; now she was on her last chance at work and she knew it.

I really wanted her to succeed. My partner (also a Christian) and I made it our goal to help her pass her three-month probation. As I've said, grace pays the price. Often I had to bite my tongue after one of her acidic comments. My partner and I tried to see Bobbie through Christ's eyes. We treated her kindly and we saw her change. She began to trust us as she realized we weren't reporting her regardless of her rude treatment. Her demeanor gradually softened. One night she even surprised us by ordering in Chinese food. Once our work was finished and the patients were sleeping, we would usually read and prepare for school the next morning. Bobbie began to voluntarily do patient checks and other mundane tasks for us so we could continue studying.

Finally, her three-month probation was up. This was it—she probably expected to be fired that day. An administrator led me into a meeting room and asked me about Bobbie's job performance. I knew if my words were negative, she could be dismissed and I would gain a new supervisor.

When you keep showing grace to someone, it not only changes the other person, it changes you too. I had grown to care about Bobbie. I knew her faults (and she knew mine), but I had also seen her good qualities. She liked to laugh. She was generous and she was a good nurse. She really wanted to keep her job.

I said I enjoyed working with Bobbie and I hoped she would stay on. The supervisor seemed dumbfounded and reminded me that my observations were strictly confidential, but I was adamant. I liked working with her and wanted her to remain the nurse on my unit. My coworker reiterated my opinion when he was interviewed.

The hospital kept Bobbie on, and she knew why. She came to trust us implicitly, and we knew we had a loyal boss. When I left that job to take a pastorate, Bobbie cried. She even threw me a farewell party. I have prayed that God would bring other grace-givers into her life.

I learned much about grace at that hospital. I realized it was not just the patients who needed it, but the staff, too. So many people grow up in graceless homes where they do not experience forgiveness or even basic kindness. Many are trapped in graceless marriages or have suffered the pain of divorce. Having rarely experienced grace themselves, they don't know how to show it to others. When they do receive grace, they don't know how to respond.

Who better to share God's grace than His church? Unfortunately, we miss many opportunities because we don't recognize them.

GRACE-GIVERS

So where does grace come from? Of course the Sunday school (and correct) answer is "from God." Christians are ambassadors of grace. Who better to share God's grace than His church? We Christians should know all about grace. Many times we do serve as Christ's representatives and extend loving grace beyond our church walls. Unfortunately, we also miss many opportunities because we don't recognize them.

I occasionally do an informal, unscientific survey of restaurant servers. I ask who their best and worst customers are. Many will say the hardest people to wait on are the Sunday "after church" crowds. They are often impatient (sitting through a long sermon can make you hungry), and they are notoriously chintzy (maybe their tithe cleaned out their pockets). By the way, nothing is worse than leaving an unbelieving server a gospel tract *instead* of a tip. Christians aren't the wealthiest people in the world, but we ought to be the most generous.

When I was in university, I worked three summers for a bricklaying company. The crew would often engage me in vigorous debates about my faith, since none of them were believers. While I could counter their arguments and critiques, I struggled to respond when they claimed their worst customers professed to be Christians. They charged that clients who were most vocal about their faith were frequently the most demanding; they sought to get something for nothing and they insisted on perfection. While I was sure they were exaggerating their case, it saddened me that their impression of Christians was so negative.

A GRACELESS TESTIMONY

My wife used to work for a company that made prefabricated building products and cabinets. Her boss was not a Christian. He used to talk about an obnoxious customer named Bill. Several times her boss cursed as he hung up the phone and complained that Bill had changed his order again. Bill would call and give Lisa's boss a tongue lashing for work that did not meet his standards. Although Bill constantly sought ways to pay less, he made frequent unreasonable demands. As her boss vented, Lisa had to agree that Bill sounded like a real jerk.

One day Lisa was walking over to the warehouse when she saw a familiar man drive into the lot. He was a Sunday school teacher and a youth leader at her church. Lisa headed over to greet him, but her boss stopped her.

"Don't talk to that guy," he said. "That's Bill. I'll handle him!"

Lisa started to explain that she knew the man, but she stopped herself, turned around, and walked back into the office. At that time Lisa was a new believer, and the revelation about Bill left her shaken and saddened.

Scripture assures Christians we can persuade the world of the validity of our message by the way we demonstrate grace. The apostle Peter urged Christian women married to unbelievers to show grace to their husbands. Peter claimed the husbands would become convinced of the truth of God's word by their wives' conduct (1 Peter 3:1–6).

Paul and Silas were beaten and imprisoned though they were innocent of any crime (Acts 16:23–34). Their prison guard was likely a tough guy, indifferent to their sorry situation. After all, he saw prisoners suffer all the time. In the middle of the night, an earthquake shook the jail and the prison doors were flung open. The warden assumed his prisoners had escaped, so he prepared to kill himself. (Roman law demanded the death penalty for losing a prisoner.)

We can persuade the world of the validity of our message by the way we demonstrate grace.

Who would have blamed Paul and Silas for seeking their escape and leaving their guard to his miserable fate? They owed him nothing, and fleeing made perfect sense. At that moment, however, their gracious response forever changed a man's eternity. These two men of faith remained in their cells. The guard was so amazed he immediately asked how he could become a Christian. By the next day his entire family had been converted and baptized. Grace is a magnetic force that draws people to God, the source of grace.

GRACE IN LITTLE THINGS

Last year the Lord convicted me that I needed to be more generous. One small way He prompted me was to tip shuttle bus operators at the airport. I fly somewhere almost every week, and I leave my car in long-term parking and take a shuttle to the airport. I noticed the drivers receive few tips. Theirs is a rather monotonous, sometimes physically challenging job, as they lug heavy suitcases in and out. So I began to store money in my computer bag to be sure I always had a tip ready.

Last fall I suffered an excruciating, persistent pain in my right shoulder. My injury was impervious to pain medicine and the discomfort was constant. In December I traveled to Mississippi to speak at a church, and I returned home to the Calgary airport close to midnight. I painfully pushed a cart with my heavy computer bag and two suitcases to the shuttle pickup area. When the bus arrived the driver opened the door and remained seated, bundled up in his warm jacket. (It had snowed several inches and the temperature had dropped dramatically during my absence.) Although I am right-handed, I had to awkwardly use my left hand to haul my heavy luggage up the stairs onto the bus. The driver watched as I trudged up and down the stairs, shivering in my light jacket and carrying my load one piece at a time. He never lifted a finger to help.

Once I sat down and we were on our way, I realized I had taken no money from my computer bag for the driver's tip. Then cynicism slithered into my brain, *Why should I tip him anyway? He did nothing to deserve a tip. This man shall go tipless.*

Of course the Holy Spirit immediately stepped in.

Holy Spirit: I thought you were going to be a generous man who showed people grace?

Me: But he doesn't deserve grace!

Holy Spirit: If he deserved grace, it wouldn't be grace.

So I dug through my bag and found some money. It pained me to be magnanimous to a selfish man. But at God's prompting, I determined that my benevolence would not be based on another person's actions but on my own "generous" character.

We pulled up beside my car, and he again remained glued to his seat while I clumsily unloaded my luggage, one piece at a time. As I prepared to take my last suitcase, I smiled at him and dropped a generous tip into his hand. "Have a great night and a wonderful Christmas!" I said.

I looked at my car in the darkened parking lot, and my heart sank. Six inches of fresh snow had accumulated on it. I wasn't sure I even had a snow brush in my car. Then I heard footsteps behind me, and I turned around to see the shuttle driver bounding down the steps of his bus and briskly making his way toward my vehicle. "Let *me* get that for you, sir!" he said. He had an industrial strength snow sweeper and he began vigorously brushing the deep snow off my vehicle. Within a few minutes he had cleared all my windows, wiped my headlights, and even swept off my sunroof. When there was not a flake of snow remaining, he turned and said, "*You* have a great night and *you* have a merry Christmas!" With that he leapt back into his bus and was off.

I was dumbfounded at the transformation. My tip had not

been *that* generous. I suspect he was taken aback at the unexpected kindness, and it stirred in him the desire to reciprocate. As I drove home God affirmed to me the joy of giving. I found deep satisfaction, not merely in the driver's response to grace, but in the very act of giving it. It felt good to give something that was undeserved. The blessing was perhaps more mine than his (Acts 20:35).

GRACE AND AN AIR CONDITIONER

A friend of mine, Rick, confessed he had been furious with his non-Christian neighbor for installing central air conditioning in his house and positioning the noisy units next to Rick's deck, and far from his own patio. Now when Rick had a barbeque he could hardly carry on a conversation over the noise from next door. He stewed about his neighbor's lack of consideration for weeks until he could hardly be civil to him. Then the Lord convicted Rick that he had allowed his neighbor's selfishness to rob him of his graciousness as well.

Why are Christians so often surprised and even hurt when unbelievers don't treat us in a Christlike manner?

People who are not born again cannot live like Christ because Christ is not living in them. Why then are Christians so often surprised and even hurt when unbelievers don't treat us in a Christlike manner? It would greatly increase our capacity for patience if we could accept the fact that we operate on an entirely different set of values than nonbelievers do. Please don't hear me say unbelievers cannot be nice people or that they never show kindness. I'm talking about a deeper issue here.

Here are a few ways Christians erroneously respond to unbelieving family and friends:

- A Christian employee gets angry when his atheist boss makes fun of Christianity.
- A Christian couple can't understand why their unbelieving parents don't support their call to international missions.
- A Christian husband is baffled because his non-Christian wife would rather take the kids to the zoo than to church.
- A Christian businesswoman is shocked at the loose ethics of her business partner.
- A Christian college student criticizes her roommate for her loose moral standards.

A PROPER PERSPECTIVE

Scripture is clear about natural human tendencies when the Holy Spirit does not dwell in a person:

> Now the works of the flesh are evident, which are: adultery, fornication, uncleanness, lewdness, idolatry, sorcery, hatred, contentions, jealousies, outbursts of wrath, selfish ambitions, dissensions, heresies, envy, murders, drunkenness, revelries, and the like. (Galatians 5:19–21a)

Paul did not mean every sin listed is manifested in every person. Don't look at your dear little neighbor lady out tending her flowers and shrink back in revulsion at her "secret vices." Paul did declare that you "were dead in trespasses and sins, in which you once walked according to the course of this world, according to the prince of the power of the air, the spirit who now works in the sons of disobedience" (Ephesians 2:1-2).

Let's not be naive. Sin is so pervasive no one is immune to its consequences. It makes people vulnerable to destructive habits and perversions. Even those who sincerely desire to overcome their sinful tendencies find their own strength is no match for sin's power (Romans 7:23). There is only one way to escape sin's bondage. We must be spiritually crucified with Christ (Galatians 2:20). Our base human nature must "die on the cross" before Christ will live out His life through us.

One reason Christians fail to show grace to unbelievers is that we subconsciously believe everyone should share our values. We Christians tend to form our own subculture. We spend most of our time with other Bible believers. We develop a common lingo and lifestyle. When we interact with those who do not accept Christ's teachings or His Lordship, we are flabbergasted. The reality, though, is that unbelieving people can be expected to act only one way—as unbelievers.

Non-Christians do not necessarily believe in an afterlife. If this life is all there is, then temporal things are much more important to them than they should be to a Christian. If they accept Charles Darwin's evolutionary theory, they may base their lives on survival of the fittest. Then power matters a great deal. If people do not believe in God's providential care, why shouldn't they look out for themselves and aggressively go after what they want? If there is no God and no final judgment, then why not live as one pleases? Worldly behavior from unbelievers should not surprise Christians; it is perfectly consistent with their worldview. Millions of people have not found salvation in Christ. Their future is uncertain, so they live for today. Rather than being

Unbelieving people can be expected to act only one way—as unbelievers.

alarmed, we should be motivated to share with them the hope of Christ and His grace.

GRACE AND A CASSEROLE

My wife is not on friendly terms with mornings. One day things were not going well as Lisa tried to get three kids ready for elementary school. No one could find their clothes, their homework, or their shoes. She frantically rushed them to school and hurried them into the building, trying to be inconspicuous since she had not showered and had her pajamas on under her coat. After depositing each child at the proper classroom and gushing her apologies for being late, she rushed back toward her car to go home.

As she passed by the staff parking lot, she noticed Daniel's teacher just pulling in. The frazzled woman was clutching books and papers as she made her way toward the school. Her tardy arrival could have invited jokes about keeping "teacher's hours" or having to go to the office to get a "late slip." It might have prompted a legitimate question about who was watching her classroom full of students. But something in the teacher's manner alerted Lisa that this woman was in bad shape.

Lisa called out to her (her name was Judy), and asked if she was OK. Judy was a single mom with two children, one of whom was autistic. A few years earlier her husband had been unfaithful to her and abandoned the family. Judy had been raising her two boys alone and teaching full time. She told Lisa that she had been awakened in the dead of night by a strange sound. She had rushed to her son's room to find him convulsing in a seizure. She had raced him to the emergency room of the nearest hospital and spent the rest of the night with him. She had finally returned home, quickly prepared herself and her kids for the day, and then rushed off to school. She was on the verge of collapse.

Lisa had a busy day planned (as all young moms do), but she could not misread this overt invitation from God to help her son's teacher. She went home and baked a casserole and a pie, then went to the store and bought treats for the boys and flowers for Judy. Late that afternoon, she rang Judy's doorbell and announced that dinner was served. Judy was stunned. Lisa explained that every day Judy cared for our son, so it was our turn to reciprocate. Lisa didn't preach a sermon or present an apologetic for the Christian faith. The meal spoke for itself. It said "grace."

The world is populated by hurting people. Most of us have been betrayed in some way, just as most know the sting of rejection. Tragically, countless numbers have known abandonment and abuse at the hands of those they trusted. As a result, many are preconditioned to expect deception, pain, and disappointment, but not grace. Gifts of grace are like ointment on a wounded soul. They bring delight and relief. They give life.

The world is populated by hurting people. Gifts of grace are like ointment on a wounded soul.

GRACE IN THE LUNCHROOM

I was speaking in a church in the Midwest, and on Sunday evening I talked about how the world craves God's grace. I declared that God is at work all around us, seeking to bring His grace to people's lives.

Bob was in the congregation that evening. As he listened he thought to himself, "Well, this preacher has never been to my workplace. It is certainly in desperate need of grace, but I haven't seen God at work for the twelve years I've been there."

I closed my message with a challenge: The congregation should look to see where God was at work around them as they went into their weekly routine the next day.

Bob was skeptical but he liked a challenge. His spirit felt oppressed by the carnality and irreverent way his colleagues acted and spoke. Although Bob had his doubts, he was willing to look for anyplace God might be at work in his corporation.

Bob was extra attentive to every phone call or interruption throughout the next morning, but nothing seemed to smack of divine activity. By noon Bob had begun to relax and conclude he had been right; God was not at work in his company. He joined some friends in the lunchroom and engaged in small talk. Suddenly he noticed a man sitting alone at another table. The Holy Spirit prompted Bob to leave his friends and join the solitary man. "How's it going?" Bob asked as he sat down. Bob wasn't ready for the response.

The man had been suffering through a rapidly deteriorating marriage. He and his wife had been constantly fighting and yelling at each other. Both felt trapped in a loveless, vindictive, accusatory relationship. They had both lost hope that anything could save their disintegrating union. That morning the man had left for work furious at his wife. He could not stand her anymore. When he returned home that evening, he planned to pack his bags and leave for good. All morning this man seethed with anger and pain. The marriage that once brought joy was at an end. He wondered how he would tell his children he would not be living with them anymore.

Bob panicked. Across the table from him was a man desperately in need of God's grace, but Bob didn't know what to say. He decided to invite his colleague to attend the service that evening. He explained that the speaker was addressing the very issues he was facing and that maybe he'd find help. To Bob's surprise, the man agreed to come. Bob offered to take him out for dinner and then drive him to the church. Once again the man agreed.

Throughout the service Bob fervently prayed that his struggling colleague would respond to the gospel message. During the altar call, however, the man remained impassive. Disappointed, Bob drove the man back to the company parking lot to retrieve his car. This man was about to go home and dissolve his family.

As his colleague thanked Bob for the evening and began to leave the car, Bob asked, "Before you go, tell me something. Did you hear *anything* tonight that was helpful?"

The man paused for a moment and then said, "It was all helpful. I want everything that speaker was talking about."

"Why didn't you go forward at the invitation?" Bob asked.

"That was my first time at your church and I didn't know if I could," the man replied.

Bob mustered his courage and asked if the man would like to pray with him right then. He could seek God's forgiveness for his sins. He could pray for healing for his hurtful past and invite the Holy Spirit to enter his life. He could ask Christ to be Lord and Savior of his life. There in that darkened parking lot, Bob led his colleague into a relationship with Jesus Christ that would forever change his life.

"Bob, thank you," the man said, "but I have to go now. My wife needs to meet her new husband!"

I heard this story the following morning. Bob was ecstatic. He had allowed God to direct him to someone whose family desperately needed a touch of God's grace. Bob's joy was obvious and he was eager to walk with his new friend through the healing of his marriage.

Dispensing Grace

Some people have known only heartache and brokenness. They have suffered criticism, abuse, and ridicule all their lives. When someone endures this kind of pain and that person has no hope in God, life is a miserable existence. Grace is a gift. Grace brings hope and joy. Grace mends what is broken. Grace reconciles relationships. Most importantly, grace draws people to God.

As you interact daily with people, keep these things in mind as you seek to share grace:

- People who have not experienced God's saving grace have no means of sharing it with others.
- Sin is the antithesis of grace. An unbeliever is ruled, however subtly, by sin.
- Sin blinds people to their need for grace.
- Many people have grown up in a graceless environment. They don't expect grace and may even mistrust the one who shows it.
- Showing grace disarms sin. Bitterness won't grow where forgiveness dwells. Anger can't take over when kindness flourishes.
- Grace is attractive just as criticism is repelling.

Every day you'll encounter people longing for a touch of grace in their lives. Like Bob, you may not initially recognize the opportunities to dispense grace, though you are surrounded by people craving what you have to offer. Make it a daily habit to ask God to help you see people as He sees them. When God reveals His redemptive activity around you, you'll have the privilege of joining Him as He sets people free by His wonderful, amazing grace.

7

BECOMING A
GRACE-GIVER

ENRY TANDEY was one of Great Britain's most deco-
rated soldiers during World War I, winning his nation's
highest military honor. On September 28, 1918, during the clos-
ing days of the war, Tandey was serving in the Duke of Wellington's
regiment at Marcoing, France. Tandey, a private, displayed such
bravery during the skirmish, he was later awarded Britain's most
coveted military medal, the Victoria Cross. During the heat of the
battle, a wounded German soldier came into Tandey's line of fire.
He aimed his rifle at the enemy soldier, but Tandey could not bring
himself to pull the trigger. Tandey showed mercy instead. The man
he spared was Lance Corporal Adolph Hitler.

When Hitler became Chancellor of Germany in 1933, he had
historians research the British accounts of the battle at Marcoing
and learned it was Tandey who had led the attack against his pla-
toon. In 1935 Hitler obtained a print of Fortunino Matania's

famous Marcoing painting depicting allied troops and hung it in his mountaintop getaway in Berchtesgaden, as a reminder of the mercy he received. When Hitler hosted British Prime Minister Neville Chamberlain at Berchtesgaden in 1938, he allegedly pointed to the picture and claimed, "That man came so near to killing me I thought I would never see Germany again." Upon his return to England, Chamberlain telephoned Tandey and passed on Hitler's personal best wishes.

On December 1, 1940, during World War II, the *Sunday Graphic* interviewed Tandey after the German air force mercilessly bombed the city of Coventry, killing scores of innocent civilians. Tandey was asked how he felt about having shown mercy to Hitler. He replied, "I took aim but I couldn't shoot a wounded man...so I let him go. If only I'd known what he'd turn out to be. When I see all the people, women and children, he has killed and wounded here in Coventry I'm sorry to God I let him go."

PAUL'S EXHORTATION

Christians have received divine clemency. We are under an enormous obligation to daily live out our gratitude for God's extravagant grace. The apostle Paul put it this way:

> Remind them to be subject to rulers and authorities, to obey, to be ready for every good work, to speak evil of no one, to be peaceable, gentle, showing all humility to all men. For we ourselves were also once foolish, disobedient, deceived, serving various lusts and pleasures, living in malice and envy, hateful and hating one another. But when the kindness and the love of God our Savior toward

man appeared, not by works of righteousness which we have done, but according to His mercy He saved us, through the washing of regeneration and renewing of the Holy Spirit, whom He poured out on us abundantly through Jesus Christ our Savior, that having been justified by His grace we should become heirs according to the hope of eternal life.

This is a faithful saying, and these things I want you to affirm constantly, that those who have believed in God should be careful to maintain good works. These things are good and profitable to men. (Titus 3:1–8)

Clearly, every human being is prone to destructive attitudes and habits. The Bible never glosses over this reality. But when He saves us, God places His Holy Spirit within us. Before salvation we were nothing like Christ. At the point of our spiritual rebirth, God begins to transform us to reflect His image as humanity was originally designed to do. As Christians, our calling is to live in a manner worthy of Christ's name. The way we treat others is a direct response to our understanding and acceptance of God's grace. The ramifications of this truth are immense.

The way we treat others is a direct response to our understanding and acceptance of God's grace.

WHAT DO WE DO NOW?

It is disheartening to realize that in spite of God's abundant goodness to us, we have been miserly in blessing others. Our failure to show grace is not necessarily a matter of being mean or nasty; it's often a symptom of our ignorance. We all have blind spots, and sometimes these can lead to disastrous consequences. For example:

- A husband has nagged and criticized his wife for years. Now she wants a divorce and he finally wakes up to the ugliness of the way he has treated her.

- A father has virtually no relationship with his teenage son. That son is now in rebellion, responding to years of his father's apathetic parenting. Now dad desperately longs for a second chance.

- A pastor watches his congregation steadily dwindle and wonders why. A deacon gently points out that he has preached God's judgment for years, coming down hard on the sin in his flock. But when his people needed grace and forgiveness, the pastor didn't know how to respond.

- A longtime Christian realizes one day that she is a joyless and cynical person. She has always blamed her circumstances (or other people); now she knows the problem is her own unresolved anger and bitterness.

- Morale in a manager's company is low. She realizes she has routinely pointed out mistakes, but her managerial style has lacked grace and praise has been sparse.

- A man's aging parents are a constant source of irritation to him. He doesn't want to hear about their problems or their aches and pains. He forgets how many hundreds of times *they* listened as he shared his worries and challenges.

- A woman experiences conflict in all her relationships. She has repeated misunderstandings with family, friends, and coworkers. She wonders why everyone else is so hard to get along with.

BECOMING A PERSON OF GRACE

All of us have areas in our character that need refining. Certainly we could all be more diligent in showing grace to one another. Even now, God's Spirit may be convicting your heart of two things: (1) behavior in your life that is graceless (critical, unforgiving) toward others, and (2) an apathetic attitude that keeps you from seeking out opportunities (or ignoring the obvious ones) to be a grace-giver. Ask God to illuminate for you specific ways to improve the way you relate to others. As you consider and pray about becoming a person of grace, here are five steps (this kind of book always has steps) to help get you on your way.

1. Consider the Source of Grace.

Everyone is capable of showing kindness to others, but grace originates from God. Most people are not naturally gracious. If you don't believe me, open your Bible to almost any page. You can't simply decide to start blessing people and then consistently do it. To give grace you have to be a person of grace, and for that to happen the Holy Spirit must be working freely in your life.

If you're a Christian, don't assume your conversion automatically made you a person of grace. There are many graceless Christians. The key is allowing the Holy Spirit to work in us to produce grace as only He can. We must learn to think as God does (1 Corinthians 2:10–16). The Bible gives numerous examples of how God thinks. Below is a small sampling from the Scriptures:

"And it will be that when he cries to Me, I will hear, for I am *gracious*" (Exodus 22:27).

"I will be *gracious* to whom I will be gracious, and I will have compassion on whom I will have compassion'" (Exodus 33:19).

"But You are God, ready to pardon, *gracious* and merciful, slow to anger, abundant in kindness" (Nehemiah 9:17).

"The LORD is merciful and *gracious,* slow to anger, and abounding in mercy" (Psalm 103:8).

"The LORD is *gracious* and full of compassion" (Psalm 111:4).

"Surely He scorns the scornful, but gives *grace* to the humble" (Proverbs 3:34).

"Return to the LORD your God, for He is *gracious* and merciful, slow to anger, and of great kindness" (Joel 2:13).

"So now, brethren, I commend you to God and to the word of His *grace*, which is able to build you up and give you an inheritance among all those who are sanctified" (Acts 20:32).

"But where sin abounded, *grace* abounded much more" (Romans 5:20).

"For you know the *grace* of our Lord Jesus Christ, that though He was rich, yet for your sakes He became poor, that you through His poverty might become rich" (2 Corinthians 8:9).

"Let us therefore come boldly to the throne of *grace,* that we may obtain mercy and find *grace* to help in time of need" (Hebrews 4:16).

Scripture clearly testifies to God's gracious character. That is the essence of His nature. Where He is at work, grace *will* abound. When He expresses Himself through your life, those around you will experience His grace. While unbelievers may be kind, they cannot match the dimensions of grace that come from God. No moral resolve or good intention will make you like God. Only Christ, living out His life through you, can make you Christlike.

I once knew a guy named Ken whose life was plagued by anger. His father had an explosive temper that kept the household constantly on edge. Ken hated the discord that filled his home, and he vowed that *his* family would never endure such torment. Yet, when he got married and the couple began having children, Ken discovered to his horror the same bitter anger that ravaged his father was also rampant in him. Although he dearly loved his wife, he would suddenly fly into a rage because of something she did or didn't do. He would find himself shouting at her and crushing her with vindictive words. His children also felt the sting of his outbursts.

> *Only Christ, living out His life through you, can make you Christlike.*

Ken was a Christian, and he felt deep remorse for the pain he regularly inflicted on his family. He would apologize to his wife and promise to do better. He often prayed and asked God to forgive him for the way he treated his family. In weaker moments he rationalized that he could not help himself, for anger was the model under which he grew up. Despite all Ken's promises, explanations, and efforts, things grew worse. His vitriolic episodes intensified as did his tearful apologies. He would tell his wife he needed her help to get better. He begged her not to give up on him. People in the church prayed for him and tried to help him, but little improvement was evident. Ken was disgusted with his behavior, and he grew more and more depressed at his weakness and inability to change.

Then one weekend his rage intensified to the point of physical abuse. His outburst terrified his wife and children, and with the help of some friends, they moved into a safe house. This devastated Ken. He desperately repeated the same promises he had uttered countless times before, but his wife told him she and the kids were afraid of him and they would not return until he was set free from his anger.

Ken had finally hit bottom. In despair he called on one of the pastors in his church. He promised to do whatever was necessary to be freed from the curse that plagued him. In a posture of deep confession, brokenness, and tears, Ken wept before God and confessed he was helpless to deal with the sin in his life. He had been trying to manage his anger, but you can't manage anger. You have to get rid of it. God was not interested in helping him *control* his anger; God wanted to *crucify* his anger so it had no power over him.

God began a mighty work of setting this man free. I saw his pastor's wife at a conference several months later and asked about him.

"You should see his eyes," she said. "He's a changed man!"

And he was. God had set him free. God's grace restored Ken's family.

Grace comes from God. You can't manufacture it yourself. God will not force it on you. It's a gift, and if you will receive it, it will change your life.

2. Consider Your Own Need for Grace.

John Newton will be forever associated with grace. His story is well known. His mother died when he was a child, and as a young man he began recklessly pursuing immoral pleasures. He drank and caroused his way through years of depraved living, eventually becoming the captain of a slave trading ship.

Then God got his attention through a violent ocean storm. Newton turned his life over to God. He went on to become a minister in England. He wrote the famous hymn, "Amazing Grace," an autobiographical tribute to God's saving work in his life. Newton lived to be eighty-two years old. As his health and his memory began to deteriorate, he confessed to his friends: "My memory is nearly gone; but I remember two things: that I am a great sinner, and that Christ is a great Savior."

We need God's grace every day and amazingly, every day He freely provides it.

John Newton understood that God's grace did not come in one installment on that stormy day at sea. He knew God poured out His grace continually for the rest of Newton's life. One of the biggest mistakes a Christian can make is to lose sight of that reality. We need God's grace every day and amazingly, every day He freely provides it.

3. Consider Other People's Need for Grace.

We are far more forgiving of our own shortcomings than we are of others' faults. We know all the extenuating circumstances and history for why we behave badly in certain circumstances. Yet as a rule we can think of no acceptable reason why our friends or spouses or children behave as *they* do. Our own daily dependence on God's grace ought to teach us that everyone needs grace. It's human nature to jump to conclusions and assume motives for what others do. It's also easy to become so engrossed in our own lives we overlook people who could use a word of encouragement or a touch of kindness.

My parents are two of the most generous people I know. They regularly give sacrificially to a wide array of causes. I was speaking about giving grace recently and my dad happened to be in the service. The following week he told me God had convicted him that he lacked diligence in finding ways to be generous and kind toward those who needed it. He asked God to show him practical ways to show grace. A couple of days later he was in a traveler's lounge at the Atlanta airport. He noticed a man cleaning garbage cans and collecting empty glasses. Dad sensed the Holy Spirit prompting him to encourage the man. So he went over to the custodian and put some money in his hand.

"Sir," Dad said, "I use this lounge almost every week, and I always appreciate how clean and tidy it is. It occurred to me that I have never thanked you for the great way you and your colleagues take care of this place. I just wanted to express my thanks."

The man was speechless. He seemed moved by my dad's words and gesture. "No one has ever told me that before," he stammered.

As my dad recounted the incident, he said, "You know, son, it dawned on me that I am around people all the time who could use encouragement, and I realize there is a lot more I could be doing about that."

Here is one of the most giving people I know discovering new and unique opportunities to extend grace.

If you consider those around you as fellow life travelers, all in need of grace like you, you will relate to them differently. If there are people around you who have been irritating or angering you, don't ask God to change *them*. Ask Him to adjust your perspective. It will radically transform your relationships.

4. Ask God to Fill Your Heart with Grace.

We have already concluded we cannot consistently act with grace on our own. Grace is God's domain. What we can do is open our lives up to God so He fills us with His love and mercy. Then we can bless others.

Many people could share life stories that would break your heart. It is incomprehensible how deeply people hurt other people. The victims of betrayal, abuse, and neglect often ask the hard questions:

We cannot consistently act with grace on our own. Grace is God's domain.

"My husband cheated on me for years before abandoning the kids and me for another woman. How can I forgive him for that?"

"My father has never said a kind word to me. He abused me as a child. He still thinks I will never amount to anything. How can I possibly show him grace?"

"My business partner embezzled from our company and sank our business into enormous debt. I've spent years paying back the creditors while he went free. After all these years, he has finally acknowledged his wrongdoing. How can I forgive him?"

The answer to all of the above is this: You *can't* forgive them. It is humanly impossible. Only God is loving and gracious enough to do that. Ask God to forgive that person *through* you. It sounds simplistic, doesn't it? It appears impossible too, but it's entirely possible with God. I've seen God do miraculous work through ordinary people as He freed them from their anger and bitterness and helped them forgive the unforgivable.

Not long ago I had the privilege of visiting a Muslim country in the Middle East with my son, Mike. We stayed with friends in a gated community protected by four security officers stationed in a small building at the compound entrance. We arrived at midnight to an unusual greeting. As our driver pulled up to the guardhouse, James, the chief guard, approached our vehicle sporting a huge smile. He greeted the driver and then, spying me, he called out, "Richard! Welcome!" Then he looked in the back seat and exclaimed, "You must be Michael! Welcome!"

Our hosts told us James was a Christian who had come from Sudan to get a job. For the next week, every time we came or went, James emerged from the guardhouse with a broad grin and greeted us as dear friends. He always brightened our day. This man radiated joy.

On our last day in the country, we bought a large tray of pastries and brought it to James to thank him for his kindness to us. He was gracious and humbly gave the glory to God for whatever he'd done to help us.

Later, I learned the rest of James's story.

During conflicts with Muslims in his country, he had lost his home and business. Because he was a Christian, none of his Muslim countrymen would give him a job. He had been forced to immigrate to the Middle East where he found work as a security guard. He worked twelve-hour days, six days a week. He spent all day sharing a guardhouse with three devout Muslim men. He slept in a small room with one of his colleagues. Because he earned less than $2,000 a year, he had not been allowed to bring his wife and three children with him into the country. If he remained at his job for two years, his company would give him a short visit with his family.

At one point a high-ranking Muslim leader had approached James with a handful of money and offered it to him if he became a Muslim. James had adamantly refused. "After all," he said, "I am a Christian. How could I renounce Christ after all He has done for me!"

Mike and I marveled about James on our flight home to Canada. We had no idea his life was so full of hardship. By the way he smiled and visited with us and talked about the Lord, we assumed he was a man seeking to better himself in a wealthy Middle Eastern country. This man had every reason to be bitter and angry. He had lost everything he owned. He had been separated from his wife and children. He worked seventy-two hours a week for poverty wages. Yet the joy of the Lord radiated from him.

Opportunities to give grace abound, but we have to ask God to remove the blinders from our eyes.

That isn't natural. It's divine. How did James maintain his joy and his hope? How did he forgive those who had taken advantage of him and oppressed him? He would tell you the answer—God's grace. God's presence in James's life was so real and personal that he was aware of every good gift God gave him. His life had not been easy, but it had been blessed by God. James had not lost the wonder of what God's grace had done for him, and it showed by the way he reached out in kindness to others.

5. Look for Opportunities to Share Grace.

Grace-givers look for practical ways to show kindness to others. All around us are people needing grace, but we can't help them if we are oblivious to their need. Our natural tendency is to be ever on the lookout for what will benefit *us*, not others. We tend to monitor whether people are treating *us* properly, rather than looking to see how we can give an undeserved gift to someone else.

Opportunities to give grace abound, but we have to ask God to remove the blinders from our eyes. If we ask the Holy Spirit to free us from self-centeredness and to bless others through us, He'll show us things we haven't even imagined. That's what God will do—but then it's up to us to respond to God's invitation.

Being a person of grace takes practice. And the sooner one begins the better.

Several years ago Lisa and I took an inventory of the many blessings we had received from God. One of them was our home. We had plenty of room for guests, so we wanted our home to be a channel for God's blessings. We asked God to show us if there was a struggling family He wanted us to encourage. Out of the blue, a pastor from another province called and told me he and his family were disheartened. They were working hard in a small church with little help. They could not afford a vacation although they longed for rest.

We invited them to have a holiday at our house. We made plans to feed them, pamper them, and give them time to relax. I gave explicit instructions to our kids, who were then quite young. We told them the family coming to our house was tired and dis-couraged. Our children were to share their toys with the pastor's kids and to do what they could to help cheer up the family.

The pastor had a four-year-old son who was suffering the effects of the stress on his family. He was, to put it mildly, a hand-ful. One day our son, Daniel, ran up to Lisa and loudly complained, "Jonathan just broke my sword!"

Lisa quickly hushed Daniel and whispered discreetly that we would replace his toy once our guests departed.

"But Mom," Daniel said, "he broke it over my head!" And Daniel had the goose egg to prove it.

Our little boy had just learned a lesson in grace. Giving grace to others so they find healing and comfort sometimes means we "take it on the chin" (or over the head).

Daniel is a young adult now, and we've watched him learn many more lessons in extending grace. Over the years he has had to forgive friends who betrayed him, people who knocked him down, and parents who failed him. When Daniel was eighteen, he was asked to preach at our church's annual Youth Sunday. He delivered a powerful message about how God's wonderful grace had sustained him through some arduous times. Then he shared how God used those hardships to channel specific gifts of grace to many others through him.

As he related the suffering he had endured and testified to God's love and grace, his sermon electrified the congregation, evoking a deep response from many people. For weeks afterward, he received notes, e-mails, and phone calls telling him that through him God had worked miracles of forgiveness and emotional healing in the members of his church family.

God is teaching each of our children, through unique personal experiences, what it means to be a person of grace. It has been a gratifying and humbling process for this dad to watch, especially since I have also been the frequent recipient of their grace.

CHALLENGE

All Christians believe in grace. But we don't all practice it. Don't let grace remain merely a doctrine to you. Let it become a lifestyle. If you are not sure whether you have a problem giving grace to others, perhaps you need to take a personal audit. Jesus said there is an easy way to tell what your heart is like—listen to what you say.

"Brood of vipers! How can you, being evil, speak good things? For out of the abundance of the heart the mouth speaks. A good man out of the good treasure of his heart brings forth good things, and an evil man out of the evil treasure brings forth evil things." (Matthew 12:34–35)

If your heart is full of grace, your words will be words of grace. You won't gossip or criticize; rather you'll say things that encourage and build people up..

There are those who sincerely believe they are grace-giving people, but if they were shown a transcript of their conversations they would be appalled at what comes out of their mouths. Take time with the Holy Spirit and ask Him to give you His analysis of your words and attitudes. Borrow David's prayer:

Search me, O God, and know my heart;
Try me, and know my anxieties;
And see if there is any wicked way in me,
And lead me in the way everlasting. (Psalm 139:23–24)

If you genuinely want to know how to be more gracious, the Holy Spirit will show you.

Paradoxically, people can show grace in some areas of life but not in others. They may be gracious to colleagues but turn into raging tyrants when they get home. Christians may be generous in extending grace to fellow church members, yet behave monstrously toward restaurant servers and grocery store clerks. Just because you show grace in some areas, that doesn't mean your life is characterized by grace. Don't be satisfied until every part of your life is saturated with grace.

Besides paying attention to what you say, take note of your behavior. A powerful clue that helps you know if your actions are Christlike (and therefore grace giving) is the result of those actions. The way people respond to you is extremely telling. Often the symptoms of our gracelessness are obvious to others, but we fail to make the connection ourselves. It can look something like this:

- A mother continually criticizes her adult children and then condemns them for having no time to visit her.
- A couple maintains a list of grievances toward one another, regularly rehearsing past offenses, but they bemoan the fact that their marriage has no joy.
- A man continually provokes arguments with his colleagues, then he complains people at work are ostracizing him.
- A woman struggles with forgiveness. She has to avoid several people at church every Sunday because she refuses to speak to them.
- A couple has attended four churches in as many years. They find something wrong with each church and then feel led to move on to a better one.
- A woman has no friends and concludes her church is an unfriendly place.

CONCLUSION

I spoke at a men's retreat a while back. I didn't know the event's organizer, but he seemed to be a kind, sincere man. He obviously cared deeply for those attending the conference. He was a strong advocate of moral purity and integrity.

At the close of the conference I got to know him a bit better. He confessed that the past year had been a disaster for him. He had hired his brother-in-law to work for him in his small, private company. The brother-in-law seemed to catch on quickly and was soon making numerous impressive sales.

Then one day my new acquaintance discovered his brother-in-law had been deceiving him. Eager to please his boss, he had fabricated his sales. Every day he would excitedly report the new business he had conducted, but it was all a sham. The owner had ordered parts and supplies to fulfill numerous nonexistent orders. Now he was committed to large expenses without the sales revenue to pay for them. He immediately fired his deceptive relative. That had been a year ago. "It will be a long painful process to forgive him," the man said.

This fine man believed in grace and he advocated forgiveness, but somehow he had convinced himself this was a special situation—that he would eventually forgive, but not right now. Perhaps, little by little, forgiveness would accumulate. He erroneously assumed some things are too hard to forgive, or at least too painful to forgive immediately. As a result he endured a year of spiritual stagnancy. Refusing to show grace was taking a heavy toll on him. It didn't have to be that way. God's grace is more than able to handle forgiveness, even in the big things.

We can all be guilty of this disoriented thinking. We believe something in our heads, so we assume it is a reality in our lives. Jesus said it is the one who *does* what He says who loves Him, not the one who *believes* what He says (John 15:14).

Do you believe in grace? Awesome!

Are you practicing it?

If you have not been the person of grace you ought to be, it's not too late. You can't go back in time to undo graceless moments in your past. But you can give grace today. Ask God to forgive you for your previous graceless behavior. Then ask Him for an opportunity to demonstrate grace to someone today.

Remember, grace never gives up on you. Grace always offers hope. Let God do a fresh and dynamic work of grace in and through your life today. He will richly bless you as you seek to be a blessing.

Study Guide

Common wisdom says any sermon must have two parts: the "what" and the "so what?" Knowing what the Bible says is crucial. Equally important is responding to its truths in daily life. This guide will assist you personally and in a group to meditate on and to consider how God wants to adjust your life in response to the truths presented in the book.

For each chapter there is a set of questions under the heading "Individual Study Guide" and questions under "Group Study Guide." Both are meant to help you process the material presented in this book. The key word is *guide*. Only the Lord knows the specific ways He wants to work in your life. If you choose to work through the questions, whether individually or in a group or both, do not limit yourself to them as if this were a final exam at school.

Individual Study Guide

Ask God to direct you to areas in your life that need to change. Be prepared, because what He reveals may surprise you and it might be painful. Take your time—this is not a questionnaire to be completed. You may need to linger over some questions longer than others. You may want to reread some chapters and study relevant Bible passages.

GROUP STUDY GUIDE

If you choose to explore grace in a group setting, here are a few suggestions:

1. Form or join a group in which you feel comfortable and free to participate candidly.

2. Choose a leader who will facilitate honest, redemptive conversation. The leader should not teach the material but should draw out insights God has revealed to the group members that week. The leader should also seek to keep the discussion redemptive and not a source of gossip. Prayerfully consider whether God wants you to be a group leader (see the Leader's Helps section at the end of this study guide for further suggestions).

3. Group participants should read the chapter and answer the "Individual Study Guide" questions before meeting together each week.

4. Unlike the individual study questions, the group discussion will be more structured and time constrained. While you should feel free to share your pilgrimage, be sensitive to fellow group members and recognize that they too have insights and questions.

5. As a group, understand that you don't have to "cover the material." An encounter with God is always more important than a completed lesson. Be sensitive to God's leading and show grace to one another in the process.

6. The goal of the group discussion is two-fold: (1) to learn from each other as God speaks to you individually, and (2) to go out and apply in practical ways what God teaches you.

CHAPTER ONE
THE PARADOX OF GRACELESS CHRISTIANS

Individual Study Guide

1. What is it about God's grace toward you that you find most amazing?

2. Have you lost the wonder of God's grace? How do you know?

3. Have you recently acted without grace toward someone? Why did you do that? What was the result?

4. Do you relate to others with humility? What is the evidence that you are a humble person?

5. Whom do you need to forgive? Are you withholding grace from someone?

6. What do you plan to do, starting today, in response to what God has revealed to you? Be specific. Make a list.

Group Study Guide

1. What did God say to you as you read this chapter?

2. What are some ways Christians are graceless toward one another? Why do you think this happens?

3. What does a lifestyle of gratitude to God look like?

4. Why is pride so pervasive among Christians? What is its effect on relationships?

5. What are the consequences of unforgiveness? How do we justify our unforgiveness?

6. What specific action did God lead you to take in response to the truths in this chapter?

CHAPTER TWO
GRACE: EXPRESSING GOD'S HEART

Individual Study Guide

1. Respond to the statement: "You do not truly understand grace until you have given it away."

2. Have you had misconceptions about grace in the past? What were they?

3. Have you recently been the recipient of God's grace from another person? What happened? How did it feel? How did you respond?

4. In what ways have you been receiving God's grace in vain?

5. What area in your life does God want to set free by His grace?

6. How is God, by His grace, presently transforming you to be like Christ?

7. How have you been a sponge or a conduit of God's grace? How might you move from the former to the latter?

Group Study Guide

1. What misconceptions do people have about grace?

2. Why do many people receive God's grace in vain?

3. Share some attitudes, habits, behaviors, or feelings in your life from which God wants to set you free by His grace.

4. How does a person become a conduit of grace instead of a sponge?

5. Share any new insights you have gained about grace.

Chapter Three
Grace: Bringing Life to Relationships

Individual Study Guide

1. Are your words characterized by grace? Think of some specific recent examples where your words showed grace or lacked grace.
2. What part of Ephesians 4:29 challenges you? Why?
3. How have you been victimized by "words of death"?
4. Who has spoken "life words" to you? What was said? How did those words affect you?
5. What has God revealed to you about your conversations?
6. Who are your models for giving grace? What do they do? What can you learn from them?

Group Study Guide

1. What are words of death?
2. What are words of life?
3. What have you learned about the power of your words?
4. Who are your models for giving grace? Describe them.
5. How are you going to improve at speaking words of life?
6. What did God say to you through this chapter?

CHAPTER FOUR
GRACE: BRINGING LIFE TO YOUR FAMILY

Individual Study Guide

1. Would your family describe you as a person of grace? Why or why not?

2. How could you show more grace to your spouse? Do you currently struggle to do so? If yes, why do you think that is?

3. If you are a parent, describe a time when you seized an opportunity (or missed one) to show grace to your child.

4. People often act gracelessly over things God does not even consider important. Describe a time this happened to you.

5. Do you struggle to show grace to your parents? If so, why?

6. What do you do once you realize you have failed to show grace to a family member? What should you do?

7. What changes need to take place so you will show more grace to your family?

Group Study Guide

1. Why do you think it can be so difficult to extend grace to family members?

2. What does a grace-filled marriage look like? If you are married, does this describe you and your spouse?

3. Recall a specific instance when a family member showed you grace. What effect did that have on you?

4. How do you make amends if you have been graceless to a family member?

5. How do you forgive family members who have hurt you? Why is this difficult?

6. What has God been teaching you about showing grace in your family?

CHAPTER FIVE
GRACE: SHARING LIFE WITH OTHER BELIEVERS

Individual Study Guide

1. How have you experienced grace from a fellow believer?

2. How have you experienced gracelessness from a fellow believer?

3. Why do Christians struggle to show grace to each other?

4. Is there someone in your Christian community who needs to experience grace? Will you give it?

5. How have you valued tasks over people?

6. Is your church a place where sinners experience grace? Why or why not? Is your life a part of God's grace-giving work in your church?

7. How might God use you to give grace to other Christians? Ask God to show you what you can do specifically this week to be a grace-giver. Then do it.

Group Study Guide

1. Why do Christians struggle to forgive one another and to give grace to each other?

2. How do Christians demonstrate a lack of grace?

3. How do Christians show grace to each other?
4. How is grace different from tolerance?
5. Describe specific instances that show your church to be a place of grace.
6. How does a church grow in grace?
7. What has God revealed to you about grace?

CHAPTER SIX
GRACE: SHARING LIFE WITH UNBELIEVERS

Individual Questions

1. Has God placed people around you who are desperate for His grace? (Hint: The answer to this one is "yes.") How do you think God wants to use you to share grace with them?
2. Have you been guilty of being graceless toward unbelievers? Consider some examples. What could you have done differently?
3. What are three ways you can give unexpected gifts of grace to others?
4. How does your view of unbelievers affect the way you treat them?
5. How has God been teaching you to be a conduit of His grace to people who do not share your faith?

Group Study Guide

1. Why can Christians be so graceless to non-Christians?
2. What are some practical ways Christians can show grace to unbelievers?

3. What opportunities has God given you to show grace and forgiveness to unbelievers?

4. What is the difference between being nice to unbelievers and showing them grace?

5. How can you begin showing grace to unbelievers if that has not been your practice?

6. What have you learned about giving grace to nonbelievers? How is God changing you to become more Christlike?

Chapter Seven
Becoming a Grace-Giver

Individual Study Guide

1. Considering all God has done for you, why would you struggle to give grace to someone else?

2. After reading this book, how do you evaluate your life as a grace-giver? How do you think God evaluates it?

3. What relationships has God brought to your attention that need more grace?

4. What areas in your life need God's grace to do a fresh work?

5. Do you normally view others as people in need of grace? How could doing so affect your relationships?

6. Do you regularly ask God to fill you with His grace? How have you experienced Him doing so?

7. Take a moment to audit your current relationships. Are they characterized by grace?

8. List specific practical actions God wants you to take as a grace-giver in your relationships (family, friends, colleagues, etc.). Ask God to help you do them as soon as you can.

Group Study Guide

1. Why are some Christians unwilling to give others what God has freely given them?

2. How does a person become a person of grace?

3. Why is it easier to believe in grace than to practice grace?

4. What has God revealed to you about the lack of grace in your relationships?

5. What is God doing in your life to make you a person of grace?

6. What are you doing differently as a result of what God has been teaching you?

7. Take time to pray together that God would use each of you to be conduits of His grace to those around you.

LEADER'S HELPS

As you join with others to learn more about living a life characterized by grace, remember that the Scriptures are your trustworthy textbook and the Holy Spirit Himself is your faithful Teacher. You can be confident that He will lead you into truth (John 16:13).

Here are a few foundational dynamics involved in group study and group discussion to keep in mind as you use this study guide to learn together about grace:

- The Scriptures are your textbook—not only the passages cited in this book, but also other passages the Lord will lead you to as you are open to His guidance.
- The Holy Spirit is your teacher. Be assured that He wants to reveal Himself and His ways to your life. He will instruct you through the Scriptures and also through each person in your group.

- As the Spirit reveals His truth to you, God will require adjustments from each of you. Obediently following through with these adjustments is the key to experiencing God's grace in your life.

GROUND RULES

When you first get together, consider asking the group members to agree to the following guidelines to help everyone get the most out of this group study experience.

- Talk about making a commitment to be learners *together*, and to be encouraging supporters of one another in this learning process. God's truth about grace holds potential for revolutionary life change. But many people will be willing to take such daring steps of growth only in a setting where they feel safe. Make a group commitment to accept each other unconditionally.
- Encourage each group member to do his or her best to answer all the "Individual Study Guide" questions for each chapter's lesson.

YOUR PREPARATION

As the group's leader, pray diligently about your responsibilities and for all the group members by name. Pray for the Holy Spirit to speak to all of you during your personal study time as well as during your discussion time together.

For all the participants, ask for supernatural blessings from the Holy Spirit and spiritual insight into eternal truths.

Ask for personal discoveries and breakthroughs where these are most needed in your lives.

Ask for protection from disunity, selfishness, and pride; ask for growth together in unity, servanthood, and humility.

Review all of the "Group Study Guide" questions for the chapter you will be discussing and decide ahead of time which ones you think are the most important. You know the members of your group, and you are free to focus on what you believe is most important for them.

GROUP DISCUSSION

Remember to include prayer as you begin your group discussion—not a token "Bless our time together," but a sincere request for the Holy Spirit to guide your discussion and your learning of the Father's will and purposes. Expect God's Spirit to be in control.

At some point in each week's session, allow for a time of group prayer when all the members are free to communicate with the Lord about the things you're learning together.

In the discussion, take the lead in sharing honestly from your own life. This will help encourage the others to do so as well. Talk about what you're learning, or still trying to learn, about the lesson. Keep the discussion focused on God's commands and purposes and on your personal application of them.

ABOUT THE AUTHOR

Richard Blackaby is the oldest son of Henry and Marilynn Blackaby. Richard grew up in Saskatoon, Canada. He now lives in Alberta, Canada, enjoying life's adventures with his wife, Lisa, and their three children: Mike, Daniel, and Carrie. Richard has coauthored numerous books with his father, including *Experiencing God: Day by Day, Spiritual Leadership: Moving People on to God's Agenda, Hearing God's Voice,* and *Called to Be God's Leader: Studies in the Life of Joshua.* Richard serves as president of the Canadian Southern Baptist Seminary.

From HENRY *and* MEL BLACKABY

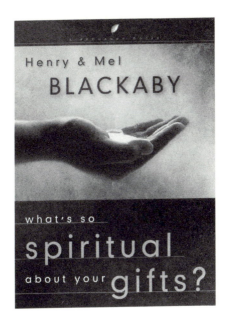

What's So Spiritual About Your Gifts?

Find out from Henry and Mel Blackaby how spiritual gifts work for the common good of the body of Christ—and learn where you fit in.

ISBN# 1-59052-344-X US $9.99
Christian Living/ Spiritual Growth/ General

From
HENRY BLACKABY

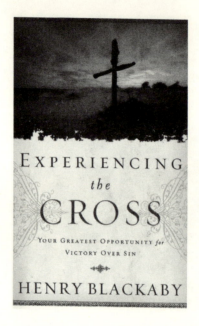

Experiencing the Cross

Blackaby swings wide the door to an intense experience
with God while coming to understand deeper
dimensions of the cross.

ISBN# 1-59052-480-2 US $16.99
Christian Living/ Spiritual Growth/ General

Also from
HENRY BLACKABY

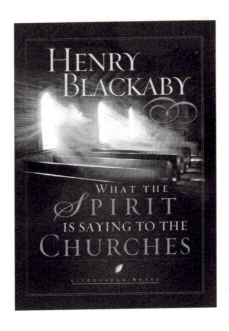

What the Spirit Is Saying to the Churches

Bestselling author Henry Blackaby teaches church lay-people how to stay sensitive to the Holy Spirit's ever-fresh guidance—and fulfill their congregation's unique mission.

ISBN# 1-59052-036-X US $9.99
Christian Living/ Practical Life/ General